Please Don't Divorce Me

Vickie Hall

Press Ahead Press
an imprint of
Rope Swing Publishing

PLEASE DON'T DIVORCE ME
© 2020 Copyright Vickie Hall
Published by Press Ahead Press, an Imprint of
ROPE SWING PUBLISHING
Illustrations: © 2020 Alexis Jester

All rights reserved. Printed in the United States of America. No part of this book may be used or reproduced in any manner whatsoever without written permission except in the case of brief quotations embodied in critical articles, reviews or fan pages.

Press Ahead Press and the logo are an imprint of Rope Swing Publishing and fall under U.S. Pat & TM

ISBN: 978-1-7342098-7-7 (paperback)

www.ropeswingpublishing.com

*This book is dedicated to my mom,
with a tremendous amount of love
and gratitude.*

Introduction

"Parents hold their children's hands for just a little while, but their hearts forever." - Unknown (Irish Proverb)

> *In our culture, more than 90 percent of people marry by age 50, and about 40 to 50 percent of married couples in the United States divorce. The divorce rate for subsequent marriages is even higher.**

If you are reading this book you are interested in approaching your divorce in a more positive manner for yourself and your children. Divorce is not pretty, but it doesn't have to be ugly either. This parent's guide is from my perspective, as a child. It is written for the benefit of children, in hopes to salvage relationships and minimize hurt for what is already a difficult time in their life. At the end of some of the chapters, I've included an "Open MIC Session" with three adults who went through divorces as children. This will allow you to hear their stories, how it impacted them, and advice they wanted to share. It is clear from the Open MIC Sessions that feelings of children have not changed over a forty year timeframe (1970-2011).

Understanding how a child perceives divorce, your words, and actions will better prepare you for what is to come with this life changing event. It will actually benefit your children and yourself. As adults, even with "the best of the best" communicators, we often times express ourselves as if the children are where we are (mentally, emotionally, spiritually), which leaves a large gap in understanding and processing a divorce. What does it mean to children? How does it impact their behavior? How does it affect them on the day-to-day?

This book will walk you through some of the major phases of going through a divorce. From the moment you decide to tell your children, through getting married again, I will provide tips and examples of what you can say to your children, what those words may mean to them, and how it affects the family dynamic.

Although it was a long and curvy road for my family during (and after) the divorce, I consider myself fortunate and blessed on how my mom handled herself, and the situation. I cannot express to you the difference she made in my life during that time. Looking back, she could have made so many different decisions, which would have changed the trajectory of my life as a child and an adult. Parents have choices to make each and every day that will affect their children. Her choice was to be her best for herself, her children, and our family's happiness.

She never wanted her children to doubt her love and support, and that is one thing I have never doubted... My mom's love for me. She never gave me a reason to. Her love is unconditional and does not have an expiration date. Love is always the answer, isn't it?

Your children want to feel confident that the love you have for them is going to remain the same. They do not want to hear negative things about their other parent. They will need to meet with a counselor or confide in someone they trust. Changes are inevitable, but explain the changes and help work through them. Children want to see your face and speak to you in between visits. They want to maintain relationships with all family members. Regardless of what they say, they do want a complete family again. When the time comes, integrate the families and make sure your children know they matter. Your children are your priority so make sure they feel like your priority. Choose love and happiness above all else and it will impact your family's lives positively.

My biggest hope is for you to acknowledge that divorce doesn't have to define who you are or who your children are, nor does it need to have a detrimental impact that lasts a lifetime. Divorce can be better than what you hear about. My family is proof that there is a better way. How you handle yourself and the priority you give your children will make a difference. It will be difficult at times, but you are well equipped to manage the divorce. You have what it takes! You may consider this time in your life as a setback, but in all reality it is a stepping stone in your journey. It is a season, and seasons change. You have the strength to endure this divorce with your eyes wide open!

*Adapted from the Encyclopedia of Psychology, American Psychological Association.

Chapter 1

"LEAVE IT TO BEAVER"

"Perfection is an illusion based on our own perception." - 101quotesabout.com

I grew up in a small town. My dad worked in operations at a chemical plant and my mom was an office manager at a dental office. We were considered middle class. My parents worked very hard to provide for our family. We had a nice house in a new subdivision, a rental property, a camp on the river, two boats, and descent vehicles. We had a swimming pool at one point and wow, the day we got a trampoline... We thought we hit the jackpot!

That was a special day! We three kids each had a $100 and we put it together to buy our first big item... a trampoline.

We went to Sunday school and church every Sunday. We were disciplined when needed, and everything was always in order around the house and in our lives. I considered our parents as strict. They wanted us to follow their rules and if we didn't there were consequences. As a child, that's strict! I remember sitting around the dinner table and whoever smacked had to sit next to our dad. If we smacked at the dinner table we got popped in the mouth. Needless to say, I never sat in that chair! I learned from Tricia, my sister, and her experiences. I have thanked God often for being the middle child once I realized the grace I received by not being the first born. To this day smacking is a pet peeve of mine and by all means, Tricia, my brother Scott, and I all have great table manners. We had chores around the house, and we were each expected to do as we were told. We knew if we didn't do something correctly a family meeting was called. "Meet in the living room in front of the fireplace," my parents would say. One of us left the laundry basket in the living room and didn't put it back in its place, and boy did we hear about it! We had plenty of rules, including but not limited to:

1) Do not call mom at work if it is not an

emergency.

2) A snack is one piece of fruit and three cookies.

3) Do not drink Mom's Tab soft drinks.

4) Do not ask to go anywhere on the weekends unless all of our chores and projects were completed.

5) Mom had to know where we were going and who we were going with.

6) Do not break curfew.

7) Honor and obey our parents.

The rules go on. We respected our parents. My mom always cooked, and we ate around the table together every night. If my dad was working the night shift, we still kept to the routine. Our lives were structured, but everything was awesome, to me anyway!

Our family had a lot of friends. I remember my parents having family and friends over to play the card games, Spades and Rook. While the adults played, the children played together. There was always a delicious meal and dessert served. Those nights were special to me because we felt foot loose and fancy free! We were able to stay up just as late as our parents, and could play outside with our friends and cousins just as long. On those special evenings we were even allowed to drink a Coke®, and that was a big treat! As I stood back and looked at the table of adults my parents always stood out to me. They were always laughing and seemed so happy.

I thought my mom was a beautiful lady and my dad was so handsome, both with gorgeous smiles. I wanted what they had when I grew up; good times, lots of laughs, and a house filled with love.

I have vivid memories of time spent with my mom, dad, and others at our camp. On many Friday afternoons, as soon as we arrived, we jumped out of my dad's blue and silver truck with our golden retriever, Wendy, and hit the water! My brother would wear his swim trunks and my sister and I would wear our swimsuits, so as soon as we got there, time was not wasted changing clothes. I am reminded of those times when I see commercials (sometimes in slow motion) and the kids and families are laughing with the sun coming in behind them, and they jump into the water from the dock and the dog jumps in, too. You know the commercials. And to think, that's really how I felt at the time; like a staged commercial that appears to be a perfect sunny day with nothing but adventure ahead! My dad built a diving board from the bank in front of our camp, which was super cool. We would run as fast as we could and jump as far out into the water as possible! We had so much fun, and I would wonder if other families "had it this good."

I remember hearing my parents talk about this special place often. They would gaze into each other's eyes, hold hands, and talk about building on the camp property when they retired. They wanted to relax on the front porch in their rocking chairs overlooking the water with their grandchildren all around them. The dream was for their grandchildren to have what we had in this very moment in time. I loved hearing their plans about their hopes and dreams. The camp…What an amazing place! It brought out the best in all of us!

Back in the day, there were not electronics to occupy our time and attention. It was each other. We played, played, and played some more. Before moving inside the city limits, we lived on a dead end street with no thru-way traffic. We ran around barefoot smashing crawfish mud houses between our toes in the ditches. We swam and we hung out in our friend's treehouse. Dad didn't buy us a slip-n-slide, but we had one! Our dad took Visqueen plastic, ran the water hose on it, added a little dishwashing soap, and we, along with all of our friends, played on it for hours. I couldn't have dreamed of life being any better for my family. You name it and we tried it. I am often reminded of those memories today when I visit my dad, as he lives in the same house on that dead end street, Bourgeois Road. How can I not smile each time I go back? I have childhood memories that have lasted me forty-four years, and hope to remember them for a lifetime. After all, these are the memories that shine the brightest before my parents divorced.

My sister, brother, and I stayed busy with our extracurricular activities and school. My brother played every sport, but baseball was his favorite. He was so small when he started playing football that the pads and helmet looked bigger than him. My sister and I both played softball for four years, but she was mostly interested in theatre, where I was in love with band and piano. Our parents were always so supportive. When we did finally come home, we would play board games and spend quality time together. I loved to bake cookies with my mom. To this day I still love baking and it reminds me of those special memories with her.

We watched reruns of a black and white television sitcom back then named "Leave it to Beaver." The suburban family seemed flawless. I tell people all of the time that we were that family. At that age, I do not recall wishing for a better life, a different life, or a life without my family around me. There wasn't anything else I desired during that time. Much to my surprise, the life I had known for nine years was about to change.

Chapter 2

THE TALK

"Good words are worth much, and cost little."
- George Herbert

The same-old famous family meeting was called. Tricia was called home from her friend's house, and Scott and I were already home. I remember going through that day and week in my mind, "What did I miss? Are all of my chores done? What is this meeting about?" Whatever they wanted to talk to us about had to have happened this week. There was no way they would let something slide from last week! My parents sat down on the fireplace. They said they wanted to talk to us about some things. Still I am wondering, "What is this all about?" They seemed so serious. I thought, "Here we go again... I have to sit in another family meeting because my sister or brother didn't do something!" You know how it goes. Just like in school, if one person acts up or does something wrong, the entire class has to hear about it. I recall in other family meetings yelling, crying, and throwing a fit that I had to listen to what my siblings did or didn't do when I did all of my chores. I tend to be a rule follower and was always too scared to rock the boat when it came to the rules, not so much with speaking my mind! I also did not want to disappoint my parents. My siblings used to say, "Vickie, if you would just say yes ma'am and yes sir, nod your head, and keep your mouth shut then the meetings would not last so long!" I could not do that. I would interrupt my parents and say, "but that wasn't me." Blah! Blah! Blah! One instance that stands out, was during a family meeting where we were asked questions and we three could not get our story straight on what exactly happened. That wasn't a good day, I must say. Our dad told us to go outside, talk about everything, get our story straight, and come back inside to give him the true story of what happened. Each time we had a different story than the last, we were getting spanked until our story was consistent with each other. Try being those kids, scared to death to say the wrong thing or get the other one in trouble! We were worried that once the truth came out we were all going to get spanked anyway. The sky was not filled with rainbows and unicorns that day!

This time was different. The room was silent and there was not any chatter. The television was not on, and I could hear the humming of the ceiling fan. I began to feel more nervous than usual. Our parents were not making eye contact and things seemed off balanced. They sat down on the front hearth of the fireplace. Dad was shaking his legs, and Mom was rubbing her hands. We kids looked at each other puzzled on what this family meeting could be about. The tension in the room was thick and the air was stale. My heart was thumping fast. Our parents looked at each other and started to speak. The first words out of my mom's mouth were, "You know how much your daddy and I love you. We want to talk to you about some changes." And after two sentences some of their words became a blur to me. Once I heard "We are going to separate," I felt sick to my stomach and the room was spinning. I was in a state of shock. I remember their lips moving, but all I could do was cry. I had the ugly cry going on with a snotty nose, bright red face, and dry heaving. I remember wanting to scream as loud as I could in hopes that it would drown out the shock, hurt, and anger. This wasn't about us breaking something, a misplaced laundry basket, or not doing our chores. My mind was racing with questions. What happened? When did things go wrong? I never heard my parents argue or witnessed them be short with each other. I found out from my sister, there was only one time she thought she overheard them in a heated discussion when she got up in the middle of the night to go to the bathroom. But at the time I wasn't even aware of that incident. I didn't understand. They are going to separate and give it some time? What does that mean? How much time? I remember my dad getting extremely outraged, but I honestly cannot tell you everything he said. I remember him yelling and his face turning red, but again a lot of it was a blur. It felt like I was in a small tunnel and once I heard certain words I shut down and the room closed in on me. Tricia recalls him standing up and saying, "No, if I leave we are getting a divorce. It's all or nothing!" He then swung his arms like an umpire calling someone safe in a baseball game. She felt like he was giving up on saving our family.

My parents separated and Dad lived at the camp. He moved back home for what seemed like a short while, and then they told us they were getting a divorce. My ears heard them say, "It's not working out." "This is not your fault." "It's between us."

And I am thinking, "Did this really happen? Have they had time to make such a huge decision? Did they try everything to make it work? What about our family?" It went by so fast. I was so confused and hurt, I believe I have blocked out some parts of my life during that time. I think it is because I don't want to remember it, none of it. It was during a time in my life where everything I knew was changing. I felt as though we all had to learn how to live in this new life, because it was never going to be the same, ever. And it wasn't. The separation went by quickly and then BAM, divorce! Did they really give it a chance to work it out (whatever that means)? I was surprised we didn't have a say in this. As a child, "working it out" meant fix the problem at hand. My older sister didn't seem to have the same reaction as me, and my brother did not completely understand what was happening because he was so young.

My world undeniably came to an end at that point. I was devastated, hurt, and angry at both of them. Not to mention completely embarrassed. What would I say to my friends? My middle school days were already feeling overwhelming enough! Times seemed tough. I was at a new school, and it was so much bigger than elementary school. My body was changing. I was trying to decide where I fit in. I felt awkward. All of the pressures of middle school, and now a divorce? From the outside we had it all, but obviously something was wrong that I didn't know about. Why weren't they honest with us? Were they being fake in front of us, our family, and friends? For how long? There were so many questions; I'm surprised my mind didn't shut off due to extreme worry.

My parents were the first couple to get divorced in our circle of close friends. I remember telling friends at school and they laughed at first, "No way, not your parents!" "Your family is perfect." It was all new to everyone around me, and I didn't know how to react or respond to them. I told them I was serious and it wasn't a joke. Then, the pity came pouring in. They apologized for what was going on and asked me a lot of questions; Questions that I was not able to answer. Like, why are they getting a divorce? Did one of them cheat? How long have things been bad at home? What did they mean, how long have things been bad a home? They haven't been! How could this happen so quickly? What a nightmare! I still struggle as I write this to describe all of the emotions and confusion I felt.

Not only was I a wreck at home, I was a wreck at school too. I lashed out at family members, fellow students, and even teachers. That year, in fifth grade, I received in-school suspension for calling my teacher an ugly name. Sadly, I didn't care though. I didn't make any excuses for myself. When I was called to the office and asked why I called her that name I said, "Because she is one." It was awful and I knew better. I wasn't raised that way, but again, I didn't care. I didn't know how to process what was going on at home, or how else to handle my emotions. I spent eight hours per day at school. There was no way I could completely focus on school work and have top notch behavior when my mind was on my family and my dad moving out. Did I say my dad was moving out? Gosh. I loved him so much and looked up to him. I trusted him. I admired him. Not having my dad at home had never crossed my mind. At the time I felt like he was here today and gone tomorrow with a snap of a finger. All I could think about during every waking hour of the day was my parents going through the divorce and how my life would change. Teachers would catch me day dreaming in class. Sometimes when I would go to the bathroom I would cry, get it out, and go back to class. At some points I felt numb and was just going through the motions at school. I was trying to imagine how tomorrow would be, and next month, and years to come. My brain was not able to fully comprehend what was transpiring. There were days when my chest physically hurt and I thought it was because my heart was broken. At nine years old, I didn't think it could be fixed. When my dad moved out, a part of my heart was gone.

Are you noticing any changes in your children? Do they have stomach aches or headaches? Are they less motivated than usual? There may be an impact with your children's behavior at school or with their school work and it is okay. Work through the issues and be patient. I am not saying to lower your expectations of your children and what they are capable of at school, but definitely be mindful of them being pre-occupied with what is going on at home and know that they need your help. Tricia was overwhelmed during this time in her life with school, trying to fit in, babysitting siblings, etc. She wanted to take her own life and thought it would be better if her life was over. She left our mom a note one night in her bedroom letting her know she wanted to commit suicide. She felt like high school was supposed to be the best years of her life and it wasn't, but mom was having hers. Mom was so happy and Tricia wasn't. I noticed a shift during this time with my mom. When I say she seemed happy that is an understatement. To me she seemed alive! Her smile was brighter and she wasn't so tense. They finally talked through this and things began to change. Thank God Tricia wrote that letter, and my mom addressed her hurt and her feelings.

> *Children who come from a home of divorced parents are twice as likely to drop out of high school than their peers who are still*

*living with parents who did not divorce.**

Throughout the book I will provide statistics and data points that I have found helpful. It is not my intention to write about the negative. It is my intention to shine a light and focus on the real issues children go through and how you can help them, so your family's relationships are not destroyed by the aftermath of divorce. Let's face it…We have all read books and articles of the negative impacts of divorce. There is so much data out there that it is overwhelming to read. I do not want your children or family to become another bad statistic. Meaning, you can help them through this so it doesn't affect their grades, relationships, trustworthiness, and self-image. I am here to tell you that I believe in you. I believe in your parenting skills. I believe you love your children. And I believe you want what is best for your children.

My parents were the first true loves of my life. I felt safe with them and in our family home. Our home was warm and welcoming, and my parents always made us a priority in their lives. I knew I could depend on them, and they were predictable, which was the best feeling in the world. I never had to worry about my parents not being there for me or not being supportive. It didn't matter what kind of day I had either. When I got home I knew they would be there and everything would be okay. I do not remember a time at this age of when I felt disappointment or anger towards my parents. When the bus would drop me off after school I couldn't wait to get inside. It was my safety net, and I could breathe. If Dad was off that day he would be home waiting. If he was working the day shift, I knew there would probably be a love note from Mom. Every day on her lunch hour she would come home and begin prepping the meal we were eating that evening. They were always there for me, always a constant, and now what? How would my routine be different than what it is now? I was completely unsure how my life was going to change and unfold. My heart was broken into many pieces and it seemed like my feelings mattered, but then again they didn't, because my parents were not going to stay together, which is not what I wanted. This was normal. Children are just that, children. They are only going to think of themselves in a general sense and only think about how it is affecting them. Children have little experience in life. They are not thinking, "Well, they love me. It will be okay. This is just about their relationship not working." If you think of the worst-case scenario of what your children may be concerned about, they have thought about it, heard it or heard something similar (relative to their age). Children will only go by what they hear from friends, what they have seen on television, read on the internet, and scrolled through on social media, unless you tell them otherwise. Even after you share positive messages with them over and over they will continue to long for your reassurance.

> **TIP.** Parents are our first true loves, so do not tell your children, "We fell out of love." or "We do not love each other anymore." Children cannot process these words or change of emotion. To them, this happened overnight, regardless of whether or not you have been having issues for a while. Children will start to question, "Can they fall out of love with me too?" This creates a nervous feeling and more anxiety of what is to come in the future with their parent/child relationship.

Initial communication regarding the divorce should be as short as possible. Let your children know there will be changes because of the divorce, and that you will both be there for them no matter what. Choose your wording carefully. Be united in front of your children. Before you meet with them, discuss what you are going to say and be prepared for anything. If their questions become too difficult, hug them and say, "We will get through this as a family."

My parents managed this well, overall. My mom kept it together although dad lost it, but there was still communication. It was heated and emotional for all of us, but I was glad we had the talk. I was so stunned by it all that I am not sure how I would have reacted if they handled it any other way. I've heard of other instances where the parents didn't talk to the children. They came home one day and one of the parents had moved out while they were at school, and the mom or dad had to tell the children alone. The parents thought it was best to avoid the children seeing the other one move out and it would be less emotional for the family. Is this emotionally healthy? Unless abuse is a factor, I would be concerned if it were handled this way. Children perceive situations, actions, and words totally different than adults, as they do not have adult reasoning. The feeling of abandonment comes to mind, as well as the children feeling as though it is that one parent's fault and the other parent was kicked out. Or vice versa, one didn't care enough to stay or to say goodbye.

Neither parent should have to endure the discussion alone. The children were made by both of the parents and it is both parents' responsibility. It is not about you at this point, as you have made your decision as a couple regarding your marital status.

In going forward, it's about the children and what is best for them. I cannot express this enough.

Children are dependents and parents are responsible for loving them, supporting them, protecting them, and caring for them in every way. With that comes sacrifices and not focused on what is easiest for you. Like my mom used to say, "The hardest thing to do is usually the right thing to do."

*McLanahan, Sandefur, Growing Up With a Single Parent: What Hurts, What Helps-Harvard University Press, 1994.

Open MIC Session

At the end of some of the chapters you will hear stories and the point-of-view from three adults who have experienced a divorce when they were children. The contributors did not read this guide before their interviews. To ensure privacy, their real names are not being used. Let me introduce you to Adam, Barbara, and Carrie. Adam was twelve years old when his parents divorced in 2011. He saw text messages on an inconspicuous phone application on his dad's phone and it seemed sneaky. Two weeks later, he told his mom. His mom confirmed his dad was cheating with her best friend. His family felt betrayed, as she and her family went on vacations with them and spent a lot of time with his family. He noticed things were changing with his dad about one year before the divorce. Adam's dad became angry and would take vacations by himself. He was distant. Maybe it was his guilt? His parents had a talk with him and his siblings. The next day, his dad spoke to each child individually. He wanted to know how each of them felt about the divorce. He assured him that he would live close by and still be involved in their lives.

> **Advice for parents: Talk to your children as a group as well as separately, as each child is different. Be careful how you say things and listen to your children. Be calm**

and cautious. As parents know, it's not what you say, it's how you say it.

Barbara was also twelve years old when her parents divorced in 1986. Her parents did not sit the children down for a talk to explain what was going on. She was plainly told that her parents were getting divorced. On the same day, her father kept her brother, then she and her mom moved out. She felt that she and her brother should have been the main focus instead of the parents fighting amongst themselves.

Advice for parents: Think about the trauma your children are going through, as their world is being turned upside down.

Carrie's parents divorced when she was a baby in 1970. They married at the age of sixteen and divorced when they were twenty years old. She and her brother were always told they divorced because they got married too young. Her father moved out of state, and she, her mom, and brother stayed in their hometown. Later, at the age of twelve she found out why they divorced. Her mom had an affair. This led to years of struggle until they both, at different times, divorced again. Her mother and stepfather divorced when she was eleven years old. There was no discussion at all. One day he was home, and the next day he was gone. This was a huge change. Her mother went from a stay-at-home parent to working full-time and going to school at night. Add the times she went out on the weekends, and there was no quality time with the children. Her abusive stepfather was out of the picture, but her mother was an emotional mess. She had to grow up quickly. She had way more freedom than kids at her age should have, which only led to trouble. She went from a student making a 4.0 grade point average (straight As) to almost failing seventh and eighth grade. She had a rebellious stage in her childhood.

> **Advice for parents: Talk to your children. By not communicating at all to them, they are left feeling unimportant and alone.**

Chapter 3

COUNSELING FOR CHILDREN

"We repeat what we don't repair."
- Christine Langley-Obaugh

Starting "Day 1" of our new way of life hit pretty hard. It was final. The separation didn't work and they were getting a divorce. Yes, my dad worked shift work and wasn't there at night sometimes, but this was different. The family unit and dynamic had changed, and this time he wasn't coming home. As a child, everything was always perfect to me at home. I couldn't understand why things had to change when nothing was wrong.

I had never heard my parents argue or be ugly to each other. There was no dark cloud that was removed from our home and that now allowed us to live in peace. Tricia once heard a heavy discussion when she went to the bathroom in the middle of the night, but it was only one time in thirteen years. I thought of saying, "If it's not broken, don't fix it!"

I continued to lash out and resist my mom as much as possible. Then, when I would see my dad every other weekend, it felt awkward. Going to the camp didn't feel like a vacation anymore. The camp was a brown and white trailer, two bedrooms, a bathroom, and a fold out couch, with a tiny kitchen. It had been so much fun before the divorce. It was our family getaway in Maurepas, Louisiana. You would have thought we were at a five star resort when we used to go there. Now, it was Dad's new home and wasn't filled with the life and joy that I was used to. It wasn't the happy place I had experienced before. The camp was a reminder to me of all the good times we shared as a family. This made things more difficult, because I compared our lives from before to after every time we saw him, and in the beginning it was only every other weekend. My dad looked sad. Mom was not there. Maw Maw Mary was not there. Our family and friends were not there. There were no more big weekends with fish fries, and we didn't have home cooked meals like with mom either. My dad was different. I could tell that he was trying to be happy around us, but he wasn't happy. I worried about him. I was scared. We would be picked up on Friday afternoons and dropped off Sunday afternoons when it was his weekend. I remember feeling the excitement of seeing him and then the devastation of leaving him. I do not have a lot of happy memories from this point forward with my dad. I know we laughed some, but it felt weighed down with gloom, and the visits seemed rushed.

The roller coaster of the separation, the actual announcement of the divorce, and then my dad moving out was crushing. Dad's laundry wasn't with ours anymore. Mom wasn't ironing his work uniforms each week. Going into their private space was a big no-no, but when I went into their walk-in closet I didn't smell his scent anymore. The drawers were empty. And, oh my goodness, his silver brush was gone. To this day when I see the same silver brush in his bathroom, it is special and brings me back in time. He has had that brush since he was a senior in high school. I have never seen another brush like it. I have told my sister that when our dad is no longer here with us on earth, I want the brush. I cannot explain it. I think it's because during those younger years it is something tangible that I remember when times were great, and I am amazed he still has it. My mom used to take such good care of him. I remember her laying out his ironed work uniforms over the laundry basket in the bathroom with that brush, shaving cream, razor, and other toiletries on the counter. When he used to get ready for work and was leaving to work the night shift, I have vibrant memories of watching him in the mirror brushing his hair. And right now, as I take a deep breath and envision those moments, I can smell the shaving cream. I remember it clumping up in the sink and him tapping the razor on the side of the sink. Those days were gone.

I had so much hurt towards both of them, and I continued to cry a lot. I used to put my headphones on and jam to my music and block out the world around me. I loved music. It was my escape and still is. On Sundays, I would listen to the "Top 40 Countdown" and tape my favorite songs on my red cassette player. I'd play them over and over again until I wore myself out, and then fell asleep. My mind would not shut off. And my heart wouldn't quit breaking.

I had gotten out of control with my sass and my mom had enough. One evening she called my dad and asked him to come over. She said I needed to go live with him since I wasn't listening to her anymore and continued to disrupt the family. I was shaken to the core. The drive from the camp to our house was approximately forty minutes. During that time of waiting for my dad to arrive, I was hysterical. The last place I wanted to go live was at the camp, the place where I once felt happiness no longer existed. I heard the knock at our back door, and Mom let him in. As he walked through the kitchen and dining room and approached me, I felt extremely small as I looked up at him. I could tell he was upset and disappointed in me. He knelt down to talk to me to find out why I was being so ugly to my mom. He said I would need to go stay with him if this was how I was going to continue to act. Part of me felt that if I lived with him he wouldn't be alone and maybe he would be happier, and part of me felt that I needed to be with my mom and siblings.

I remember holding on to Mom's leg crying and begging her to let me stay. She said, "Okay, but if it happens again we will need to make a change." I was thinking, "Why would I want to stay if I was so miserable? Why would I want to stay if I missed my dad so much? Why wouldn't I want to go with him? Why was I continuing to say hurtful things to my mom?"

Mom took all three of us to see a counselor. I'll never forget this day. I resisted and didn't understand why I needed to go see a counselor, a stranger in my eyes. He did not need to know all of my personal feelings. Why did I need counseling if my parents were the ones with the problems? I was outraged. I rolled my eyes at every mention of going, but I was happy to miss school for the appointment. She drove us into the larger city, Baton Rouge, Louisiana, about 35 minutes away. She heard he was one of the best counselors in our area. I looked him up and found that he had practiced for over fifty years. We arrived and he met with all four of us. He talked, asked questions, and then had us draw pictures of our family, situations, and feelings. I was mesmerized by his deep, smooth voice, his long, shoulder length hair, and mustache. He was so calm and seemed relaxed. I felt like my life and mind were chaotic spaces, so being in such a mellow environment was nice. I could breathe. The office was not bright at all and felt like a lounge. I felt like I was in slow motion during our first visit. At the end of the session he said, "She needs to come back." Yes, she was me, the middle child who was sensitive and vocal about her feelings. That's one thing I have never had a problem with… expressing my feelings, good or bad.

I saw the counselor for about a year and a half, every three weeks. It truly helped me process my feelings and emotions. I'm grateful my mom "made" me go. I felt like I was at a breaking point and my life was crumbling all around me. Seeing him helped me work through everything. I was glad I was able to express my feelings without being scared of getting in trouble with my parents. Since the counseling continued for a long time, he helped me work through my feelings about my dad no longer being involved in my life to the extent that he was before. I learned not to take my hurt out on others. I did not enjoy hurting my family with my words, but at nine years old, I didn't know any other way.

> **TIP.** Seek counseling for your children. Find a counselor that you and your children are comfortable with, whether it is a local practice, at church, or elsewhere. Do not allow your children to make this decision, as they do not know what is best for them. Children should not dictate adult decisions.

Children need an outlet where they are able to speak freely without worrying about being reprimanded for what they say. They also do not need to be bothered with hurting their parents' feelings. Having your children go to a counselor does not mean you are not sufficient for them. It doesn't mean you are not strong enough. You are not an expert at counseling, so seek the best for them in this specialized profession. Recognize that it is difficult for children to express their true feelings to their parents if the feelings they have are about their parents, and the situation they "got the family into."

I have heard all too often of stories where the children did not have the opportunity for counseling or didn't continue counseling as they were living through the hurt, and later in life those emotions caught up with them. I have also witnessed this of close family and friends, including my sister. It tends to have a snowball effect and the snowball only gets bigger until everything is addressed.

> *It has been shown that there are long-term effects for children if they do not get the help they need emotionally and mentally. One study shared that children from divorced homes may have more psychological problems, than children from which one of the parents has died.**

When I read this study I thought that it was an impactful observation. I remember thinking as a child that when someone died they did not have a choice about dying. I had several loved ones pass away as I was growing up. It was either caused by a tragedy, old age, or a severe illness. In my mind it was out of the person's control. However, with my parents' divorce I felt that they had a choice, and the choice was to break up our family.

When we went to counseling, Tricia did not go back after the initial consultation. She felt like it didn't involve her, so she didn't need counseling.

She obviously appeared to be okay emotionally at the time, or the counselor would have suggested that she return. She ended up rationalizing the divorce in her mind as a friend, because she heard from our mom what happened. As a child, she didn't feel like she needed any help. Unfortunately, this would later catch up with her. She was the child with the least amount of counseling during this time and has had the most amount of counseling as an adult, related to her childhood, job, and marriage. Tricia has suffered from clinical depression and been to counseling for over eight and half years.

There has been much discussion with her counselors between the parallel of our parents' marriage and her marriage. Also, was she trying to duplicate the Daddy's-little-girl relationship in her own relationships over the years? I have been intrigued by everything she has gone through and discovered. She has always wanted to be taken care of and not make decisions. Her value in her mind has not been about her, but how happy she makes others. She has also magnetized to dominant personalities in her relationships.

Our dad was dominant. And she lost herself the longer she was with her husband. Finally, after several years of counseling, she has developed more respect for herself and is willing to stand up for what she believes is right and just. Since her divorce this year, she is taking time to search for who she really is before she engages in another romantic relationship.

Take your children to counseling even if they are kicking and screaming, and regardless of whether they want to go or not. Remember earlier I mentioned parents make choices every day? Children see divorce and the situation they are in as a choice made by you, their first true loves. This gets deep, because it is deep. Even though this divorce may be the best thing to do for you, your spouse, and your children, they do not see it that way. This book is not about what you are feeling right now, the reason or justification for your divorce, or anything of the sort. It is about your children and how they are interpreting, or have interpreted, the divorce and your decision, as well as what you can do to make it better for them. You can make things better for them, and you will continue to hear this, because it is important.

*Robert E. Emery, Marriage, Divorce and Children's Adjustment-Sage Publications, 1988.

Open MIC Session

Adam attended counseling for three years, on and off. He was counseled with his family, mom, dad, siblings, and by himself. He also saw different counselors. He benefited from the counseling because he was able to talk through everything and get advice on how to manage his emotions. Eventually the counseling stopped because he wasn't getting anywhere with his dad. There was no compromising and they would end up arguing.

> **Advice for parents: Be sure to get the help your children need. Be open to compromising and hearing your child's concerns and feelings without getting defensive.**

Barbara did not receive any counseling during the divorce or after. As an adult, she believes she still has unresolved issues regarding the divorce, as it is too painful to think about or talk about to this day, thirty-two years later.

> **Advice for parents: Kids need a safe space to express themselves and speak openly about how they feel and the impacts of the divorce.**

Carrie was not given the opportunity to have counseling. She has talked with close family and friends throughout the years. As a child she bottled all of her emotions up, never wanted to complain, hurt anyone's feelings, or disrupt life in any way. She believes she would have benefited from counseling. The mark on her life from her stepfather's abuse lasted a long time, thirty-five years. As an adult she still thinks about going to counseling.

> **Advice for parents: Parents should seek counseling for their children whether they believe the child is handling the divorce well or not. This is a huge life-shift and your child should at least have a consultation or two with a counselor and see where they are emotionally.**

Chapter 4

COUNSELING FOR PARENTS

""We can choose to throw stones, to stumble on them,
to climb over them, or to build with them."
- William Arthur Ward

Parents should also seek counseling for themselves, so they are better equipped to handle the divorce, process their feelings, deal with their children, and begin to heal. This provides parents with the emotional energy and strength needed to make it through this process with their children. The stronger you are, the better you will be for your children.

TIP: Seek counseling for yourself and remember, your children are not your counselors.

Your children are not your sounding board. I repeat, your children are not your sounding board. I do not care how old your children are as you go through this divorce. I do not care if you think they are your friend. Please, please do not talk to your children for your support. Children do not want to hear about your marital relationship. Anything, and I mean anything, you say may destroy the image your children have of their mom or dad. This can spiral out of control quickly. I am certain this is a tough one to hear. There is so much time spent with your children that I understand it is difficult not to slip or "speak the truth," because you are getting blamed by your kids, or overwhelmed with the pressure of always keeping it together.

However, there must be boundaries. Growing up I always knew there were boundaries not to cross. There was a clear line of what was acceptable or unacceptable of my behavior. The boundary goes both ways. Parents also have a boundary. I understand there is a very fine line between being a friend and a parent, especially as children get older and become adults. However, no matter how old children get, they do not want or need to know parents' problems and issues in their personal relationship. It is a heavy burden to carry as a child. There isn't any other way to say it. It seems standard to tell the children what really happened years later when they are adults. Yet, it is not necessary. Children should be on a need-to-know basis with regards to their parents' relationship, and I cannot think of much that they need to know when it could impact their image of a parent. Remember, children do not have the adult reasoning and maturity that you do.

Tony Cox discusses the research and its implications of brain development with Sandra Aamodt, neuroscientist and co-author of the book, *Welcome to Your Child's Brain: How the Mind Grows from Conception to College* in a podcast.

> *Research suggests that most people do not reach full maturity until the age of 25.**

In our society, eighteen years old is often referred to as an adult. You have heard it all, how eighteen year olds are able to join the military, go into a bar, buy tobacco, move out, etc. While all of that may be true, an eighteen year old still does not have the brain development and maturity that many people would like to think. No matter how old a person is, they are someone's child and will always be someone's child. Before saying anything about the divorce or the other parent ask yourself, "Is this helpful or hurtful?" By saying the words out loud, it will be a reminder to avoid hurting your children further and confusing them even more than what they already are. Protect your children and do not deflect your hurt and opinions onto them.

My sister, Tricia, was impacted by the very thin boundary line between the parent and an older child. She was a teenager when our parents divorced, and mom thought it was acceptable to tell her everything that happened, and the truth of why my parents were getting a divorce. At the time, my mom confided in her during their nightly walks. I am certain mom felt a lot better. Sadly, that wasn't the case for Tricia. They were very close in their relationship, and I understand Mom felt comfortable sharing her feelings. However, it risked Tricia's feelings and image of my dad. Tricia felt horrible knowing some of the things shared and began to resent my dad. She also felt sorry for my mom and was surprised she stayed in the marriage as long as she did. It crushed her in the beginning. It forced her to feel as though she needed to react a certain way and take sides. She also continued to feel sorry for our mom after hearing all of the gory details. This was unfortunate. Mom regretted it later, but the words cannot be taken back or unheard once they are said. What's done is done now. Lesson learned.

I saw my parents as perfect. I remember the first time I heard my mom slip and say a curse word. I was in college at the time. I was surprised and it caught me off guard. At the time, I was twenty years old. By that time, I knew she wasn't perfect, but she was a living example of a Christian, a classy lady, a wonderful mom... my mom. For years I had my parents on a pedestal and that's how it should be. I looked up to them. I respected them. I adored them. It is difficult to describe and find the words as I write this chapter. I understand as we get older we finally realize that our parents are human! They make mistakes just like we do.

As children that isn't the case. Children are learning how to act, how to treat people, values, morals, work ethic, table manners, what is acceptable and not acceptable in general, and so much more. Parents are teachers. I rarely heard my parents say, "Do as I say, not as I do." It was quite the opposite. They were more like, "Monkey See, Monkey Do" or "Do as I do." The reason is because they were living (at least in front of me) how they were teaching and training me to be. That was the expectation. The standard was set and it needed to be. Regardless of what you say, children will believe it is "not so bad" to do the very things you told them not to do if you are doing them. You turned out okay. What can it hurt? I am sure you have heard many quotes about this subject. I love the quotes below:

"You are what you do, not what you say you'll do." ~*Carl Gustav Jung*

"I don't trust words, I trust actions." ~*Author Unknown*

My pastor preached on children and relationships with their parents. I love the way he articulated it. When children are young, they are to obey their parents and do as they are told. As they grow older, they are to respect and honor their parents. The caveat is that parents are to act in a way or live their life in a way to deserve the children's respect and honor. Seriously, let that one sink in. The caveat is that parents are to act in a way or live their life in a way to deserve the children's respect and honor. This is a powerful statement.

As a parent myself, I have to keep myself in check often in hopes that I am practicing what I preach to my children. Trust me. I have been "mom shamed" before, and it doesn't feel good. Here recently, I was talking to my son and explaining what we watch and what we listen to can affect our attitude and mood. I explained that I didn't want him to listen to certain rap music and watch certain shows that bleep all of the time. I told him that if he would listen and watch only positive music and shows for thirty days he would notice a difference. I went on further to say, "You know how momma does not like the shows that bleep all of the time…" He sat there and listened. I could tell that his mind was churning and the gears were moving. He said, "What about that show Housewives of Orange County?" I had a total mom shame moment. He wasn't being rude or condescended when he said it, but he remembered that I watched the show and it had bleeping in it in place of the curse words. We can all sit here and think that this seems silly. I am the adult and he is the child and adults can do whatever they want to do. However, my son recognized that I was doing something that I told him he should not do. Will he make better choices because I do? Will it impact him in a positive way when I do not set my DVR to record the next season? Am I willing to risk my credibility with my children for the sake of being able to do whatever I want to do because I am an adult?

When I needed to know how to do something or wondered what was best, I asked my parents to show me and observed how they acted. This starts at a very early age. When I needed to learn how to walk, my parents showed me. When I needed to learn how to potty, my parents showed me. When I needed to learn how to read, my parents showed me. When I needed to learn how to play with other kids, my parents showed me. When I needed to learn how to drive, my parents showed me. The list goes on. We always look to our parents to teach us, help us, give us advice, and guide us.

Don't change your relationship with your children because you are going through a divorce. What I mean is, the relationship has not changed. Your children are not your friends in this scenario and during this time. If you didn't talk to your children about adult problems before, why start now? If you have talked to your children about adult problems, stop. Draw a line and remind yourself not to cross such an important boundary. Your words could potentially change a child's entire image of the other parent. Do you want to be responsible for having that negative impact on them? As they get older they will blame you for anything negative that goes wrong with the other parent, because in their mind you told them the "truth." Their image and feelings of and about the other parent is based on their experiences and how the other parent treats them, not your experiences. A counselor, close family, or friend who supports you and your family is a better option. Find whatever best fits your emotional needs in order for you to be a ROCK for your children and do it. It will be one of the best decisions you will make.

*Tony Cox, Tell Me More Podcast-October 10, 2011.

Chapter 5

DON'T BE A NEGATIVE NANCY

"Positive words with good intentions behind them nurture and encourage growth. Negative words with negative emotions literally rot and destroy." - Billy Beck

When I think about the time during my life that my parents went through a divorce, what I remember most is my mom always being so positive and strong. The way my mom handled the divorce is my inspiration for this book. I had a parent that made a decision each and every day to do whatever it took to make sure her children were nurtured, supported, loved, fed, and had a safe haven at home.

She made sure we knew she loved us. There were times that things were heated and she would say, "I love you so much, but I do not like the way you are acting." She was a ROCK during all of this for my family. I cannot recall one time when she talked negatively about my dad or his family to me.

In the beginning, my dad said mean things about my mom. It was extremely painful to hear. It seemed so out of character for him. Yet, it fueled my hurt feelings. Again, I blamed them both, but hearing bad things about her made me even more angry and hurt. I honestly believe parents do not realize they are doing this to their children. Tricia witnessed dad being cruel to mom on different occasions. She couldn't understand how he could go from loving someone so much to being hateful. She joked with her friends that she wished they would have stayed together so there would be less fighting. Before the divorce there was never any fighting that we saw. After the divorce, the fighting began. Seems backwards to me. Our mom kept repeating the same message, "Your dad is hurting so he is saying hurtful things."

I believe we can all acknowledge that in any situation there is usually his side of the story from his perspective, her side of the story from her perspective, and then the full comprehensive truth. It is human nature to share our story from our perspective, with our emotions and feelings attached to the story. We all do it. In the situation of a divorce, children do not need to know any of it though. This is not a funny story to share that is embellished with theatrics and hand motions. It is not a repeat of town gossip. It is not a serious story to be told with suspense. The issues are between the parents, not the parents and children. A relationship between partners is far different than a parent/child relationship.

Children are not armed emotionally to handle these situations. I loved my dad, I trusted him, and have always looked up to him. If he is saying these things about my mom they must be true, right? My dad had never given me a reason not to trust his words. In an article of "The Power of Positive Emotions," studies revealed that individuals feel and do their best when they have at least three times as many positive emotions as negative ones. When we feel more positive emotions than negative emotions, difficult situations seem easier to handle.*

TIP: Do not speak negatively about the other parent. If you do not have anything positive or supportive to say, then keep quiet.

I would yell at my mom while we were arguing

and I threw out some things to her that my dad told me. She couldn't believe it. I could see the hurt in her eyes. All she would say is, "That's not true." "I love you, Vickie, and so does your dad." She was consistent in her messaging no matter how many times I pushed her. How was she able to be so patient? How was she able to take it?

Months later, my dad came to the house. He said he needed to speak with all of us. I was so nervous. What is he going to say? My heart was beating fast, and I was scared another bombshell was going to go off. Could this get any worse?

He sat us down where we had our family meetings. He said he wanted us children there, because he had something important to say. He apologized to my mom, in front of us, for all of the things he had said. He said none of them were true, and he said them because he was hurting. He asked my mom and all of us children for his forgiveness. This sincerely impacted me. It was powerful to see my dad admit he was wrong. I felt relieved and my flame of hurt burned a little less going forward. I also felt ridiculously horrible for believing them and using them against my mom in arguments, as well as in my heart. Emotionally, she was my punching bag. Yikes!

If your child is coming home and saying things to you that are clearly being communicated by the other parent, diffuse the conversation. Continue to be positive. Don't be a Negative Nancy. Talk to the other parent and agree not to say negative things about each other. Children do not understand when this happens. Their first two true loves, who they've always put on a pedestal, are now against each other. It's too much for a child to comprehend. The child feels like they need to blame the other one more now. Unity is the key to parenting your children, especially after the divorce. If not, your children will suffer even more. Do not give your children a reason to choose one over the other. That is an unbearable pressure. Do not ruin the image of the other parent your children have in their minds at the sake of being right or wanting to look better. Children do not care who is right or wrong. They are not interested in what happened between the two of you. They are interested in how this is going to affect them and their relationship with you. Deflecting your hurt onto your children is damaging. Your children's hearts are big enough to hold love for everyone!

*The Power of Positive Emotions, Kids Health - The Nemours Foundation.

Open MIC Session

Adam's dad was negative about his mom and her side of the family. He felt he was put in the middle.

Advice for parents: Try to stop yourself before saying negative comments. Do not vent to your children.

Barbara's parents were negative and condescending about one another, and she felt caught in the middle.

Advice for parents: Do not put your children in the middle. It makes them feel trapped feeling like they have nowhere to go and no one to turn to.

Carrie constantly had to hear condescending and negative remarks about the other parents. The parents were civil in front of each other, but not behind their backs. It made her feel uncomfortable, and she always struggled to find balance between defending one parent, but also afraid to lose the love of the other parent. Her stepmother was not all bad, but because of the way her mother spoke about her, she never allowed herself to have a bond.

Advice to parents: Get along and be genuinely kind to one another. Be a positive light in their life and show them that your love for them is what you all have in common.

Chapter 6

WHY ARE THEY CHANGING?

"Life is about change. Sometimes it's painful. Sometimes it's beautiful. But most of the time, it's both." - Lana Lang

In the previous chapter, I mentioned my dad asking for our forgiveness and his apology about saying horrible things to us about our mom. This was a change. My dad was not known to be the apologetic type. I was surprised by this action. He was someone I looked up to, but I perceived that he always had to be right and had a temper. We were scared of him when he got upset over us doing something wrong.

I recall an incident when my sister and I made

my brother really mad. I cannot remember exactly what it was about. I do remember him getting an ice pick from the kitchen and stabbing our bedroom door when we locked him out. He also hit the door with a baseball bat as hard as he could. The doors in the house were not thick and seemed hollow. My sister and I just knew he was going to break the door down. He was banging on it with his fist, yelling, and carrying on.

My mom came home from work and had to deal with the situation. She noticed right away that we had stickers and pictures we drew hung all over our door. My brother used them to cover up the holes, dents, and splinters where the door was coming apart. I could see the expression on her face. She was scared and worried and so were we. Our dad was going to flip out when he got home. Mom talked to us. She told us to make sure we bathed before going to bed and clean our rooms. She had a lot of nervous energy. I could tell this wasn't going to be good when our dad got home.

My sister and I bathed and put on our pajamas. I stuffed rolls of toilet paper in my panties and got into bed early. We laid there scared and trembling. We were scared about getting spanked and scared for our brother. We had the sheet and comforter pulled up to our ears waiting for my dad to come home.

The front door opened. We could hear our parents talking. I remember hearing my dad's voice getting upset, and the sound of his work belt being pulled harshly from his pants. The house was above the ground, so we could hear his every footstep walking towards us down the hallway. My sister and I began to cry and fear came over us. My dad slung open the door and asked, "What happened?" It was always important for him to know and he could not stand it if we lied and our stories were different. We all prepared for this that day… making sure our stories were the same. At least that meant fewer spankings. We told him the story and he yelled at us. He held that doubled over belt above his head and said, "The belt is the law," and slapped the belt down to make it snap. My sister and I were crying so hard he became blurry. Once I wiped my eyes, I saw that he broke off the light switch from our bedroom wall, and it was on our floor. It was an awful day.

The reason it is important to share this story is because my dad began to change after the divorce. He started going to a different church and was born again. In case you are not familiar with the term, born again is a phrase used in Evangelicalism as a "spiritual rebirth." He was baptized as a child, but this was basically a renewal for him going forward and committing his life to Christ as an adult. We were not seeing him as often any more, but when we did he seemed happier and more patient most of the time. More importantly, his temper was not as bad. It seemed odd to me that he was changing. He was a great man, but I remember that he stopped going to church with us when my parents were still together. It didn't seem important to him to go as a family, but now it was. He was going on Wednesdays and Sundays when he wasn't working. When we were with him we would have to go to his church and their Sunday school.

There were other changes, too. Every time I saw him it felt like a sermon was being preached. In my mind I am thinking, "Church isn't until Sunday!" When we did get to see him, I wanted to visit and talk about our lives and the things that were happening that he had missed. I did not want to be preached to. I had a pastor for that. I wanted my dad.

Then, the judgment came into play. All of a sudden it didn't feel like I was good enough since I wasn't like him. He would get all in an up roar. I remember rolling my eyes a lot! We were at one of his church's picnics, and this man kept staring at me. I told my brother and sister that it was creeping me out. Ugh! I get the chills just thinking about it. The man walked over and questioned me about the gold jewelry I was wearing. He started asking me questions and then told me that I was "worldly." The people at his church seemed so fake and judgmental.

Needless to say I did not feel comfortable there. As I looked around for my dad, he was laughing and hanging out with "these" adults. I didn't get it. Where was my dad when I needed him in that moment? He wasn't there with me for sure. I wanted to crawl under a rock and never come out. I did not feel protected. I did not feel secure. I felt scared and unwelcomed. This went on and became a bigger problem and barrier in our relationship. He would make comments that every time the church doors are open he needs to be there. Between his work schedule, church, and church events, we saw him less and less. Eventually, it came to an end except for birthdays and holidays. I'll get into that more later on in the book.

During one of his weekends, on a Saturday night, he took us to see a lady preacher at a revival. We were all sitting in this church listening to her say the same things over and over again. She was yelling, and so firm. My dad would look down the row at us. What or who is he looking for? He pursed his lips. I was a bit confused and didn't understand his reactions throughout the sermon, and it was a long sermon! It was hot, too. I cannot stand to be hot. I made it through and we were on our way home. I remember it being really late and dark outside.

Dad began to yell and his face was turning red. When he yelled, I could see spit flying out of his mouth as we passed by street lights on the side of the road. His burnt orange Pontiac was swerving. I was in the front seat and my brother and sister were in the back seat. He asked us how could we just sit there and hear the Gospel and not get up and go to the front. He said my sister was going to Hell for going to a rock concert and my brother made sports too important. He said we were not Christians. I thought to myself, "What's going on in this car right now? Are you kidding me?" My siblings were crying in the backseat and didn't say a word. I yelled back and told him to bring us home, and I was never going to his church again! I told him I was a Christian, and if being a Christian in his church was anything like him, I didn't want to be his kind of Christian. I told him to slow down and that he was scaring me. It was a horrible night.

I was more confused than I had ever been in my life up until that point. I couldn't understand why I was not good enough the way I was as his daughter? I had been good enough before the divorce. He never questioned my Christianity then. It made me think long and hard. My dad seemed better in some ways and worse in others. How could he talk to us that way? I had met many others who were on fire about God and they did not act like that. He was my dad for Pete's sake!

Parents will change during this time as they

begin to search for their happiness, discover who they want to be, and/or seek for a deeper meaning in life. It is inevitable. However, keep in mind your children are not looking for the same things as you. They are looking for you, your love, and your support just as they did before the divorce.

> **TIP:** Be mindful of how you approach your children with of any new habits and/or ways of living. Think about how you are going to incorporate those changes when you are with your children.

This chapter isn't just about a change in religious denominations, as this was one of my particular experiences, and one of the changes that stood out to me. It could be eating healthy. If all of the sudden you are not bringing your children to McDonald's every time you pick them up and now you are preparing a protein, healthy carbohydrate, and vegetable, then that is a change for them. It doesn't mean the healthy meal is not better for them, but it is not what they are used to. The same goes for exercising. The routine before may have been to get home and watch a favorite family sitcom together on the television. Now, you are telling the children that you all are going bike riding or playing tennis instead. In their minds they are thinking, "Why wasn't it like this with mom/dad before?"

Change is not necessarily a bad thing, but it is different. It could change personalities, confidence, physique, priorities, attitude, and many other traits. Change is usually for the best. Be prepared to explain why things are changing, though. I know this seems trivial, and you do not need to walk on egg shells around your children. You do not need to second guess everything you are doing as a parent either. However, children long for routine. The only routine they knew was how the family lived before the divorce, so naturally they will compare everything to how it is after the divorce. If they do not understand the reason for the change, they will assume it is only changing because of the divorce. This is the last thing you want, for your children to stack another item to their divorce pile of emotions and confusion.

Parents do not need to justify why they are making changes, but explanations would help to understand the benefits of why the changes are being made when it affects the children and their routine. Remember, the children do not have adult reasoning or understanding. They do not see the big picture, meaning they do not see that eating better and exercising are what is best for them.

My mom also changed. She was always petite in size when I was growing up, but I did not recall her exercising as much as she did after the divorce. She would walk with my sister, but now she was running a lot. It seemed excessive. To me, she looked happier in the face, but sickly everywhere else. I believe at one point she was below one hundred pounds and near zero percent body fat. As a child, I remember thinking that she was only doing it to look better for other men. You know, men other than my dad. She didn't need to have a sit down and explain everything to me and justify it, but because I didn't know why she was changing, it allowed my mind to go elsewhere on why I thought she was doing it.

In hopes to explain this further, I will use an example of how children think in comparison to your adult reasoning. Everything is compared to how life was before the divorce. It is as if everything before the decision is bulked into one category of "life before the divorce," in one bucket. Then, as each thing changes it is stacked on top as yet another change, regardless of if it is good or bad in your eyes. Below could possibly be how your children compartmentalize or sort the changes:

-Life before the divorce

-The divorce

-Parent moved out

-Visitation schedule

-A different life routine

-The way it is at mom's house

-The way it is at dad's house
-Mom is changing
-Mom's habits are changing
-Dad is changing
-Dad's habits are changing
-Flow-down changes to me
And the list goes on…

It reminds me of a pyramid, where all of the stones are being stacked side by side and then on top of one another. Visualize building a pyramid for a moment, starting with the foundation. Until the child feels whole again or normalcy in his/her mind, the peak of the pyramid is not reached. The children are working through each stone to get to the top of the pyramid. Trust me, they want to reach the top. Children are resilient and will make it through this. Understand though, that they could feel heavy and weighed down with all of the changes and trying to keep up with what is right, acceptable, or the new way. Multiply that by two, because both parents are changing.

Children only knew one way before, and now it is different. Every change appears magnified to them. Be patient.

Chapter 7

MAINTAIN FAMILY RELATIONSHIPS

""Family is not an important thing. It's everything."
- Michael J. Fox

With a divorce, comes a splitting of the extended families. I do not believe it is intentional, per se, but it happens on different levels. The parents should support each other during this transition and decide on the new way of sharing their children's quality time with both sides of the family. They still want a relationship with families on both sides, and not just at the holidays. It is hard enough seeing parents split up, so not seeing their family members as often as they are used to should not be an option. Parents should put aside their emotions for what is best for the children.

> **TIP:** Keep in contact with the in-laws (aunts, uncles, cousins, grandparents). Schedule times for you to bring the kids to visit their family members, even if it is on "your days."

The divorce is between the parents, not the family members. Stripping them away from the children because it is his/her side is not fair. By doing that you are depriving the children of sharing their love and experiences with your spouse's family, and continuing to receive love by them too. Make this another priority, no matter how hard it may be. You are divorcing your spouse. The children are not divorcing their families.

After the divorce, my mom made the effort to keep in contact with my dad's side of the family. I had cousins, aunts, uncles, and grandparents who lived locally and in Arkansas. She would bring us to see our family locally or we could ride our bikes to visit. My mom never spoke negative about my dad's family. She loved them and so did we. You cannot turn a switch off and decide there will no longer be a connection with other family members, regardless of whose side of the family they are on.

My mom and grandmother, Maw Maw Mary (on my dad's side), still maintained a relationship and remained close. They loved each other and I cannot tell you how great it felt to see that continue. It was a gift to witness. On Mother's Day each year, my Maw May Mary sent my mom flowers. We were very close to my grandmother, and I cannot imagine how I would have felt had it not worked out this way. That would have been yet another barrier I would have had to go through if it wasn't for my mom and grandmother making it important for themselves and us. My sister, Tricia, was best friends with our first cousin on my dad's side of the family, and those relationships remain unchanged. She is grateful for the bond and relationship.

Every summer, my parents would bring us to Arkansas to visit family on both sides. After the divorce, my mom contacted my dad's side of the family to let them know when we were coming. We would spend one week with her side of the family and one week with his side of the family. How amazing is that? I have significant memories spending time with all of our families.

Throughout my life both sides of the family came to special events like birthday parties, high school graduation, college graduation, etc. Now that

I have children, they do the same. I am so thankful for my family.

I do not recall any of my family members talking ugly about my parents or the divorce. The focus was on us being there and spending time with everyone. My mom told us it was important for us to continue to have this time with all of our family. I was relieved that this was not something that would change for us. I loved my extended family regardless of what was happening between my mom and dad.

It is hard for me to wrap my brain around the flip side, because this way is all I know and have experienced. My husband experienced the total opposite. His parents divorced and he never saw his dad's side of the family again. I couldn't believe it when he shared this with me. What went wrong? Were the feelings so hurt that the grandparents, aunts, and uncles didn't reach out either? What stopped any of the twelve adults involved to contact the children? I will never know the answers to these questions. I do not need to know the answers. The choices were made and it is in the past. Yet a part of him was shut off. As my boys have grown up, they ask about their grandfather whom they've never met, along with all of his family. They have so many questions about him. What does he look like? What does he do? Where does he live? Are his parents alive? There is a lot of family out there who they will never know. It is unfortunate. They have not missed what they do not have, yet in comparing it with their other grandparents and family members, they wonder. It's human nature. My oldest son has recently told us that he WILL meet his grandfather one day (my husband's dad). He is very adamant about it. He said he is willing to experience disappointment and/or be uncomfortable. What do we say? No? Not likely. He will go to college within the year. He is at the age where it matters to him. We've agreed that I will bring him when the time comes, as my husband does not want to be there. My boys will never know that side of the family based on decisions made over thirty years ago.

You love your children. Continue to do your very best to put them first. Speak positively about each other and the families. Do not allow this divorce to tear all family relationships apart. It doesn't have to be that way. Family is too important to take them for granted or lose them. Do not destroy any family relationship.

Open MIC Session

Adam's mom would schedule time for them to visit his dad's side of the family. He continued to go on a vacation each summer with all of his cousins and family members on his dad's side. His dad no longer went. He just started going again two years ago. His mom would make arrangements for him and his siblings to attend.

Neither of Barbara's parents maintained relationships with her dad's side of the family.

Advice for parents: It is the parent's job to help maintain the extended family relationships.

Carrie's parents maintained family relationships really well. She was close to her grandparents on both sides of the family. Her mother maintained a good relationship with her dad's mother. Wonderful memories were made. The grandparents also served as a buffer if she was upset about something, and they would speak to her parents to soften the situation.

Chapter 8

SHOW UP / BE PRESENT

"I will always put family first. Every time I haven't I have regretted it and apologized." - Andrew Forrest

Tricia, Scott and I were very involved in activities. I played in the band, took piano lessons, and played softball. My brother played basketball, baseball, and football. He also competed in BMX bike racing. My sister played softball, was the basketball team's manager, and was in the drama club. We were all in youth group at church as well. We were very busy. My mom was involved with the Parent/Teacher Association (PTA) at our schools.

Thinking back, I can only remember one time that my mom did not show up for one of our events. That's it. It is important for you to show up for your kids and be present at as many events and functions as possible.

I started playing flute in 5th grade, and eventually learned the piccolo. I loved being in the marching band and concert band. The feeling I got every time I performed was cool, but the most amazing part was knowing that my mom (or later, Mom and her husband, Pop) would always be watching and present for me. This continued during my entire childhood, and continues now through adulthood.

When I graduated from high school, I attended college two hundred miles away. I accepted a music scholarship to play in the marching band and symphony. My mom and pop gave up their Louisiana State University (LSU) season tickets and purchased season tickets for all four years at my college, Northwestern State University of Louisiana (NSU). This was a big deal down here in South Louisiana. Pop had been a member of the LSU Tiger Athletic Foundation for years, since he was an alumnus. LSU is a huge Southeastern Conference (SEC) school and NSU was very small. No one around here gives up their LSU season tickets. No one except my parents. They drove the seven hour round trip for all home games and went to at least two or three away games. This was all to watch me perform pre-game and at half-time, which was no more than sixty minutes total. There were over 320 band members who always knew my parents were coming. They couldn't believe it. For me, it was the norm. It didn't take long for me to realize just how special this was, and that not all parents were able to attend or did not make it a priority to attend. The entire band saw that my parents attending was a constant. They'd say, "Can't wait to see Mom and Pop!" They quit asking if they were coming and automatically knew my parents were going to be there.

Tricia remembers Mom attending plays where she was working backstage with props and lighting. It was important to Tricia, so it was important to my mom. It didn't matter that Tricia was not on stage acting and could not be seen. Her daughter was participating in something and she was not going to miss it. She doesn't have the same memories of our dad attending these events for her and being there for support and neither does Scott.

Like I said, it was the norm for me. It wasn't until I went to college that I realized not everyone had a family like ours and how blessed I was. A bunch of us girls would pile up in our dorm rooms and share stories about our lives and families. As I would look around the room out of so many girls I had met, no one had a family just like mine. They were all unique. It was not that one was better than the other, just different. I couldn't imagine it any other way, because this is what I had in my life and what I experienced. It was in this moment that I began to appreciate my parents and understand all they have done for me. I remember during my first semester of college calling Mom and Pop, crying my eyes out. They thought something was wrong, but it was tears of joy and unending gratitude.

> **TIP:** Make it a priority to attend your children's events and functions. If you are physically able to go and can take off of work, then go!

The Father Effect: Positive Effects on Involved Dads, written by Michelle Higgins for Pathways to Family Wellness, explains that involved fathers have a significant and positive impact on their children's development. In his article, "Feminist Academic," author and father, Hugo Schwyzer, sees a real change in the way that the current generation of fathers is approaching their parenting role: "Many of them see fathering as a genuine vocation. They don't just pay lip service to putting family first. They do it."

Children yearn for participation and support

in their lives. Rationalizing how difficult it is to go is not acceptable, it is simply making excuses. Workplaces typically understand and hours can be made up. Do whatever you can to show up and be present for your children. I am not saying you are not a good parent if you do not go to all of your children's functions and events. I am encouraging you to do your very best in attending, because it does matter. Whether or not your children show you their appreciation, it does matter to them. Even if they roll their eyes as you take pictures, it does matter to them. They will not fully appreciate you like you wish they would, until college, and then even more so once they have their own children. It's okay. You can handle it. You've got this!

When a child expects a parent to be there and they do not show up, it is devastating. I have seen this quite a bit in my family. Mom would send dad our schedules for whatever we had going on during each season. He came to only one of Scott's high school baseball games in four years. Tricia doesn't recall him being there at any of her events either. I remembered him coming to one performance. I understood my dad worked shift work, however, I did not understand why he wasn't there when he wasn't working. My dad did not get sick often either. I really wanted him there. I expected him to be there like before. The closer someone is to us, the higher the expectations are in that relationship. So for parents, from a child's perspective, the expectations are high!

I interpreted this lack of support as a lack of my importance and that he didn't love me as much as he used to. Children do not understand any adult reasoning. You have heard me say that a lot and it cannot be repeated enough. You will hear it again. They only see it as he/she is not there for them. What else is more important than your children? Who else is more important than your children?

During my senior year of high school, I experienced a feeling I had not felt in a while. I was performing at half-time, and for one song we were still and not transitioning into other formations. I looked up in the stands and saw my dad. I began to tear up and missed some measures of music. I was in shock. He was there watching me. Now, to some this may seem minor, but to me it was exciting, because it was a rarity. I always did my best, but I wanted to do it even better once I saw him. I can't explain it really. I felt a since of relief. With my teary eyes looking out I thought, "He does love me."

Once I got home after the game, I was still on a high from seeing him be there. I thought to myself, "Okay. I believe I have forgiven him." That's the level of emotion I was feeling. I went on and on to Mom and Pop. They were happy for me too. Why was this such a big deal? I ended up lowering my expectations of my dad based on his pattern of not being there. I did this to avoid the disappointment I felt when he wasn't there for me at something that was important. So, when he did show up it was an influx of positive emotions I wasn't used to feeling, the high.

Then the guilt poured into my heart. The guilt of being excited to see my dad in front of my parents who were always there for me. It was an awful feeling. As I got older, I remember crying to my parents about this guilt when I would see my dad and be happy about it. I didn't want to diminish everything they had done for me or all of the times they showed up. They calmed me down each time and told me they wanted me to have a relationship with him and were happy for me when he was around.

The parents that show up are taken for granted in a way, but that's a good thing. Children know they can always count on them being there, so it's a given, and one less thing they have to worry about, and that's how it's supposed to be. Children rely on their parents to meet their emotional, mental, and physical needs. It's the same concept as when we were babies. When we cried as babies, we cried to have our needs met. We were either hungry, ready for a diaper change, had gas, feeling sick, or some other ailment. We began to rely on our parents to be there each time we cried. We then expected our parents to be there each and every time we needed something. We expected them to be there, hence the expectations were introduced and set for us from that point forward.

We have all seen after school special television programs, movies, or other dramas where the child waits on the porch or in the driveway for the parent to show up because they said they would, and they do not show up. They even have this story line on my favorite channel, Hallmark™. You know the drill. You have seen the kid's disappointment. You are better than that. I believe you will show up as often as you are able. I do not believe you will intentionally break promises. If you say you will be there, be there.

Children need their parents' support in all things. When they do not feel supported, they do not feel loved by the parents or important to the parents. Children will remember when you are there, but it really stands out when you are not there. It is for you to decide how they remember you.

Open MIC Session

Adam's parents both attended his activities until after the divorce. His dad no longer showed up for him. It made him feel awful and unimportant.

> **Advice for parents: Be there for your children. If you can't show up tell them why. Give them reassurance that you love them and want to be there.**

Barbara's parents did not attend her school and extracurricular activities or events.

> **Advice for parents: It is very important to stay present in the children's lives.**

Carrie's parents were always there for the important moments in her life, even with her father living 300 miles away.

Chapter 9

STAYING CONNECTED

""A connection is the energy that exists between two people when they feel seen, heard, and valued; when they can give and receive without judgment; and when they derive sustenance and strength from the relationship." - Creating a Life Inspired

When I was growing up, the standard visitation schedule after a divorce was for the mom to have full custody and see the dad every other weekend. I cannot express to you how foreign that felt to me. Transitioning from having my dad home every night, other than when he worked nights, to now every other weekend was tough. Before the divorce when he worked the night shift, we spoke to him in the evenings. I remember thinking, "Would I still speak to him every night? Was I able to see him in between visits? That seems long." Long it was.

I would get excited to see my dad when it was his weekend. I'd pack my clothes and things for the weekend and wait for him to pick us up. It just felt odd some weekends, though. He didn't seem as upbeat as he used to be. As I mentioned earlier, going to the camp was not the same anymore. It seemed so serious now. It felt like we were not connected. Sometimes we would go longer in between visits if he had to work. Then the number of visits became less and less. If one of us children had plans, he wouldn't come pick up the other two. Scott remembers Dad calling and telling him that he wasn't picking him up since my sister and I were not going. This has now been designated as the day my dad quit. The day he gave up. The day he no longer fought to spend time with him. That is how Scott felt. He loved seeing my dad and going to the camp. He loved to fish, run trout lines, and go frogging. He didn't care if Tricia and I weren't there. He wanted to spend time with our dad.

As children get older, especially teenagers, their social lives take off like a rocket. In middle school, there are football games on Thursday nights. In high school, it is "Friday Night Lights" baby. Mix in all of the practices and school work and the schedules become busy. So for us, every other weekend became every two, three, or more. It then dwindled down to every now and then plus birthdays and holidays.

I don't remember talking on the phone often with my dad in between visits. That was long before there were cell phones, so the calls would need to be made once he got home via a landline or from work. There wasn't FaceTime so a lot of times I wouldn't see his face until his weekend came. The switch from seeing my dad all of the time to every now and then was rigid. There is no other word for it. There was a void and the bond diminished over time. My heart continued to break.

When we got together, all three of us would talk, talk, and talk, as we were trying to catch him up on everything going on in our lives since the last time we spoke to him or saw him. It seemed like a lot of energy was spent catching him up rather than true family time, like we had before the divorce. Each one of us was always trying to get a word in.

As time went on it felt like I didn't matter anymore.

TIP: Stay connected with your children. Call them as often as possible, even if it's just to say, "Hi, I love you! How was your day? Good night and sweet dreams!"

Parents, it is your responsibility to stay connected. Please do not let yourself get so down, that you begin blaming your children for not calling or reaching out. Do not take the easy way out based on inconvenience and chose not to see your children. Do not allow yourself to believe that your children do not want to hear from you or see you. Children are going to be aggravated with you at times, not like you sometimes, think you are too hard, think you are dumb, and much more. This will happen regardless of whether you are married or divorced. Do not allow yourself to think that they feel that way because of the divorce. They feel that way because they are children. Do not give up and throw in the towel because of their social lives, inconveniences, and teenage hormones. It would mean the world to a child to receive a phone call every day, or every other day, saying the simplest things; a five minute call. With today's technology, there really is no excuse a parent can give that would justify not contacting their children in between their visits. I am also very thrilled that the visitation schedules are much different than from when I was a child. The frequency and duration of the visits have increased. There are several people I know that have 50/50 custody. That is wonderful!

Children need to feel wanted by their parents. Do your best not to withdraw from your children. Remember, children do not have an understanding of adult reasoning and feelings, but they do feel the effects of them whether good or bad. Reba McIntyre and Kenny Chesney released a song in 2007 called, Every Other Weekend. It describes the parents' feelings and routine of every other weekend. The dad feels like they are a family again for fifteen minutes, and the mom doesn't know what to do when it is quiet and the children are gone. It is a beautiful duet and I encourage you to listen to it.*

When I first heard this song, I cried my eyes out. Still today I will tear up. My dad felt like he was losing his family every time he dropped us off, and my mom told me when I got older that she swore she heard our voices when we were not with her. Knowing their feelings now makes this song that much more relatable to what my parents experienced. It also reminds me of all the hurt being experienced by families dealing with divorce across the world. When I see parents meeting in parking lots in our town and doing the drop off and pick up, I think of this song. The parents were in love, married, had children, and now their entire world is turned upside down. I have not met a family yet that didn't hurt from a divorce, regardless of the reason that the parents are no longer together. No one wants to see their family unit separated.

The good news is that you can make a difference during and after this divorce. You have the strength within you to be the parent you were before the divorce, or maybe even better! I encourage you to be as much a part of your children's lives as possible no matter what the visitation schedule is. Make it happen for not only your children's benefit, but for yours. Stay connected!

*Songwriters: Connie Harrington / Connie Rae Harrington / Skip Ewing

Open MIC Session

Adam's mom called or texted every day when he was at his dad's house for visitation, but his dad did not contact him in between visits. After the first year, Adam no longer went to his dad's house. He was abused. It was miserable being around his dad and stepmother. After that, it could be months in between calls or text messages. His dad felt like it was Adam's responsibility to keep in touch.

Advice for parents: It is your job to stay in contact with your children.

Barbara lived with her mom and didn't have any visitation with her father. She also had no relationship with her father. He never contacted her again.

Carrie spoke with her father on the phone often enough. She spent every summer and each holiday with him. She felt their relationship lacked the closeness and love other friends had with their fathers.

Chapter 10

DATING / RE-MARRYING

"Remarriage is like driving a car. Too much looking in the rear view mirror at your past, and you will crash." - Brian Mayer

When my parents started dating, it was definitely a weird feeling down in the pit of my stomach. Just the thought of my parents being with other people made me sick. How would this change our lives again? Will they like us? Do they have children? For years, I even fantasized about my dad and mom getting back together.

I never met anyone my dad dated until he was ready to marry Veda, the woman he was in love with.

My mom dated a little, but she made it clear that we were her #1 priority and that would never change. One example is that she turned down a weekend trip with a man at his fancy house somewhere. She told him, "I have my children this weekend." The man couldn't believe that she wasn't going and couldn't make other arrangements for her children. She told us, "I want to spend every bit of time I have with you."

When I looked at my mom, I started seeing her differently as I got older, and she became happier. She seemed more confident. She laughed a lot more. She changed careers. Soaking wet she weighed 100 pounds, but was a superwoman. She took us on vacations by herself. One summer, the four of us went to the beach. My brother had a cast on his leg from a baseball injury. We walked from the condominium and across the street. He used his crutches, but once we got to the sand she carried him. She didn't want him to fall or get sand in his cast. He was a muscular boy, too. Now, when I look back on that vacation and have visions of her carrying him, it reminds me of an Arnold Schwarzenegger movie. You know, where something blows up, he saves someone, picks them up, and then carries them off to safety? I am not kidding. She definitely did it all.

In January of 1987, my mom started dating a man named Jimmy (now known as Pop). Oh boy was I resistant to it once I realized they were seeing each other every chance they got! He then started coming over every day. I began to lash out again. I would say sly remarks and occasionally be disrespectful. Not to mention the time I said, "You are not my dad!" Ouch! I wasn't ready for my life to change again. It was too soon for me still after three years. I thought, "Just when things are getting settled, it is changing again." I was worried about all sorts of things and situations. Was he being nice now and would he change later? Was my mom really happy with him? I didn't know she was unhappy with my dad for so long. How would I know this time? What is his family like?

He started coming to our events and functions. He was thoughtful, patient, kind, and compassionate. On Valentine's Day, the month after they met, we walked outside and each of us had a heart hanging from the patio by the back door. There was a special message on our hearts. When my science fair project was coming up, he helped me. It looked perfect. He helped us with our homework each night if we had any questions. He would play board games with us, go hiking, bowling, watch movies, and do other fun things with us. As time passed, I fell in love with Pop. I felt like our family was becoming whole again. I felt like I was reaching the top of my pyramid. He would never sleep over, but he would stay late almost every night to hang out with us and Mom. About nine months into the relationship, I was practically begging them to get married. Of course, they told me that these things take time and although they loved each other, we all needed more time together. I didn't understand it at the time. Was something wrong? If they loved each other, why wouldn't they get married since we were okay with it? Are we a problem? Does he think we will become a problem?

What seemed like forever passed by and then Pop proposed to Mom in front of his family at Mulate's, a Cajun restaurant. When we got home from Dad's after the weekend, we were all together that evening. He said, "I've asked your mom to marry me. Now, I'm asking you to marry me as well. I am not here to replace your dad. Please know I am committed to marrying all four of you as a family." It was such a sweet and memorable moment that I will treasure for a lifetime. He was dedicated to making all of us happy. I was so excited! The biggest stand out for me is that Pop chose to say yes, not only to my beautiful mom, but to us. He did not feel obligated to take care of us, he wanted to take care of us and be in our lives forever.

TIP: Take time to integrate your children with your

> future spouse and their families. This should not be rushed. It shows the children how important being a family is and that everyone knows each other and feels comfortable and accepted.

I was nervous once we started going to his family's holiday celebrations and events. It took some time for me to get adjusted to all of the new people. His family was loud (just like me), fun, and had traditions for everything. Things seemed okay, but we only saw them at the holidays and sometimes in between.

My uncle was getting married soon and his fiancée' had a son. One evening, I was in Granny's (Pop's mom) kitchen talking with her, my sister, and my soon-to-be cousin. He asked her, "Once my mom marries Mike, will I be able to call you my grandmother?" She said, "Oh heavens no!" I didn't know what to think. My mind was racing. I was already referring to her as my grandmother and my parents were not even married yet…that's how much I loved this woman. I was crushed. I found my mom and shared this with her. I began to cry and told her I didn't understand. I was hysterical. I thought his family liked us. I thought Granny loved me. Would this ruin them getting married now?

Later that night, Pop came in to wake us up. He said, "I'm sorry, but we are leaving." We lived two and half hours away. I didn't know what was going on and why we needed to leave so abruptly. We were getting all of our things together to load into the car. Granny was crying asking Pop not to leave. She wanted to sit down and talk. We were all standing down the hall and I heard him say, "Mother, they are my family. This is my white picket fence dream. If you cannot accept that I am marrying all four of them, then we do not need to come back." She apologized and said, "No, please stay. I understand."

When we left at the end of our stay, Pop shared more details with us and said that Granny always dreamed he would get married, have children of his own, and live happily ever after. Marrying a divorced woman with three children wasn't in her dream, but he assured us that we were his dream.

As each visit came and went, we became part of their family. I felt like I belonged. We were at the mall with Granny and she introduced me to one of her friends as her granddaughter. I cried when I told my parents. They were happy tears. Prior to that, I was introduced as my mom's daughter.

It took time for all of us to become integrated. My parents knew what was best. Not marrying right away was the best decision for our family and gave us all the time we needed. To this day, I am very close to Granny. Just a month ago my Pappy (her husband) passed away. It has been very difficult, because I love them so deeply. We have spent every holiday with them for the last thirty-two years. My grandparents were married sixty-six years and were together since junior high school. Their marriage has been an exemplary example to everyone who knows them, and it was apparent that their families, especially their three sons, were a priority in their lives.

Phenomenal moments occurred just a few weeks before Pappy passed away. He had been battling the awful disease of Alzheimer's over the last two years. It is one of the most horrific diseases I have witnessed to date. At the age of 85 his physical body was, what I consider, in top notch condition. He had asthma, but was overall healthy. The only major surgery he had in his lifetime was for his cataracts, and he was not on any significant medications. Unfortunately, as the disease progressed his mind stayed behind. My husband, Jim, and I went to see him as he was coming near the end of his life here on earth. We visited with him and Granny for a few hours. During our time together he would come in and out, and I would see and hear glimpses of him and his true character. We laughed, and laughed some more! Out of the blue he looked around the den and said, "You know, Audrey and I have been married for 66 years." He then pointed to the crown molding near the ceiling around the room and said, "I think it would be neat to have a picture from every year we've been married hung in here." I looked at Granny and thought I would lose it at that point. She smiled at me. I told him I would do that for them if he wanted me to and order all matching frames. It would look like a border. He giggled and looked down. Before we left I knelt down in front of him to ensure our eyes met. I put my hand on his knee and told him I needed him to know that he and Granny have everything Jim and I desire, and we look to them as a sound example of marriage and family. He responded with his childlike grin and voice, "Really?" I got choked up then, but kept the tears from rolling down my face. I said, "Really!" I told him I loved him and in that moment I knew it would be the last time I saw him.

The following week he continued to decline. The hospital bed was already brought in, and Granny had Pop and my Uncle Mike move the single bed from the extra bedroom right next to him in the den. My sons went to visit him. My oldest son, Brandon, couldn't wait to share what happened during his visit. On the Sunday morning he and Pappy were talking. He said he enjoyed having the time with him. He was in shock about what happened next.

He said, "Mom, Pappy looked at me and told me to take care of you, Dad, and Nathan." He looked me dead in the eyes and said, "I know we are not blood, but Brandon, you are my great-grandson and I love you." Brandon was extremely touched by this moment. He continued, "Mom, I am 16 years old and Pappy has never told me he loves me! I always hug him and tell him I love him, and he says, "Good boy" and smiles. Mom, he knew who I was and what he was saying."

I want to repeat Pappy's words, "I know we are not blood, but Brandon, you are my great-grandson and I love you." Think of your future and imagine how you want it to be. How do you want your children to feel about you? Do you want your future grandchildren to feel this level of commitment and love regardless of this divorce, and whether or not you are blood related? This divorce goes beyond you and your children. The decisions you make now with your children will affect the future. Imagine how you want it to be and do everything you can to make it your reality!

In 1989, over two years after they started dating, Mom and Pop were married. It was an awesome day! We were officially a family! I felt like I could breathe again. I know it sounds strange, but it was a huge relief. I missed having a whole family at home.

As I mentioned, I didn't meet any of the women

my dad dated. In 1990, at my Maw Maw Mary's Christmas party, I met Veda for the first time. Dad seemed excited to introduce us to her. She was quiet, but very nice. Dad seemed happy.

On January 31, 1991, less than two months later, we received a call from Dad. My sister answered the phone, spoke, and then said, "You need to tell Vickie and Scott." So I got on the phone and he said, "What did you think of Veda? I said, "Well, I met her that one time and she seemed nice." He said, "What do you think about me marrying her?" I said, "Ummmmmm, I guess time will tell." He said, "We are getting married by the Justice of the Peace tomorrow at the courthouse, and I wanted to know what you thought of her." My heart fell to my toes and was pounding. My eyes filled up with tears not only about this news, but the next day was my brother's birthday as well. Part of his call was also to tell my brother he couldn't bring him to his annual birthday dinner.

This was another change occurring in my life. I was sixteen years old at this time. When we would go over to their home I didn't feel welcomed. It felt like we were visiting instead of going to our second home. I never slept over there again. Who was this stranger? Where does her family live? Who are they? Do they have family traditions? It was just too much for me to process. I was extremely angry and hurt. We didn't have the opportunity to get to know her, her family, or have the integration with them as a couple, much less a family unit. I only had Mom and Pop's way of doing things to compare it to, and it was completely different. I assumed if they did it that way, Dad and Veda would too.

It was hard to see my dad act so differently with Veda as well. He would speak softly and in a little baby voice when he was flirting. He would open her doors. He was so accommodating. Why couldn't he be this way when he was with my mom? What made her better than my mom? Since we did not have the integration process with Dad and Veda, the family dynamic was completely different than what we had at home. I felt betrayed and unimportant.

It didn't matter that we didn't see him as much as we did in the beginning. What mattered was that he was my dad, he got married, and this was just another decision I had to accept. It was a big pill to swallow. You would think that I wouldn't be surprised, but I still hung on to the hope of feeling like a family with him again at some point as well. This change just made that possibility even more difficult.

This was a struggle for me. I already felt like my dad had drifted away and it felt even worse after they married. Why was it bothering me so much? I didn't see them that often. He was happy with her. I was happy with our family. What was the problem? It bothered me because he was my dad, and I was still his child. I cannot describe it in greater detail than just that way.

Throughout the years I never spoke to my dad about this. It was his decision and his life. I came to a point in my life where I had to accept that he was never going to be the dad he was when I was a young child. I held on to an image of my dad for so long, and I had to let it go. Those years were gone. Pre-divorce dad was a totally different man with a totally different life now. I had to accept him, his wife, his life, and our relationship for what it was.

It wasn't until I was twenty-five years old when we had our father/daughter dinner a few weeks before my wedding that this issue was brought up. We shared a lot that night. He asked me if he could ask me questions about things. I guess since I was getting married he saw me as an adult, but I am not quite sure. Maybe it was because so much time had passed and he felt safe to ask me. One of his questions was, "Why don't you children have a relationship with Veda like you do with Jimmy?" This was a question I didn't think I would ever have to address and quite honestly, I am glad it was asked several years after it happened. My feelings were no longer raw and I had moved forward. I didn't have a lengthy response either, "Dad, you and Veda did not share your life with us or even try to be a family. We met her one time before you married her. With Mom and Pop, they dated for over two years, and we became a family. That was the difference." I further explained that you cannot become a family with a stranger.

I have a wonderful relationship with them now. It just took longer for the integration and years after they married. I needed to get to know her. It went from loving Veda because she made my dad happy, to loving her for the special woman she is and our bond now.

In this area, things came full circle when Dad and Veda renewed their vows in 2016, in front of family and friends. It was their twenty-fifth wedding anniversary. It was a special day for me to witness their love and commitment in front of God, family, and friends. I let Veda borrow my pearl jewelry, and took pictures to capture their day. They both looked amazingly happy!

I do not believe everyone will agree to what I say next. Let me say first, that I do believe a husband and wife's relationship comes first, and then immediately following, the children come second. A lot of mommas may not like to hear that. I get it. I am a momma bear, too. I have been happily married for over twenty years. My husband and I have always had God in our relationship and we make our relationship with Him and each other as our priority. Our relationship comes first, in order for us to be the best possible parents for our boys, whom God has entrusted to us. That is my true belief. I've seen the flip side to where the children and their schedules become such an overpowering priority over the parents' relationship that their relationship suffers. The kids go to college and they look at each other across the table and do not know each other. They were going through the motions. I am not going to go deep into this subject, but I believe it is important to consider as you move forward.

I also believe if you divorce and have children from that marriage, your children should come first. It is a dramatically different circumstance when you marry and do not have children. Once you divorce, I do not believe the same rules apply since you had children first and already have a family, before your next spouse comes into your life. It sounds contradictory I know, but at least in the beginning it must be this way. Your children were entrusted to you by God before the subsequent marriage. As a parent, you have already made a commitment that must continue to be fulfilled. There is no excuse for a parent to abandon the obligations of taking care of his/her children and making them a priority.

Once the family is integrated and established then your new spouse can come first. It is damaging to the parent/child relationships when the children do not see themselves as a priority in a parent's life. You may believe it is a crazy thought, but I have seen it all too often, and not just in my family. If you want a complete family again and for it to be a happy one, then the children must be considered a priority as well.

When "love is in the air" and you are excited to move on to the next chapter with your future spouse, please know that sacrifices may need to be endured until your children feel comfortable. It will benefit your family long-term. Isn't it worth waiting until it is right for the entire family?

Open MIC Session

Adam's dad dated the woman he had an affair with and they married in 2014. He felt so betrayed by this woman, and he's never had a relationship with her. There is still a significant amount of hurt. When his mom dated he was excited for her and wanted her to move on. He said it was good to see her "get out there." She's never gotten serious with a man yet and it has been seven years.

Barbara felt unimportant when her parents started dating. Her father remarried when she was thirteen. Her mom never remarried.

Carrie's mother began dating immediately after her second husband. It was a nightmare. She was going out every Friday and Saturday. For two and half years she dated a man that was awful...not much better than her first husband. He made Carrie cry daily and tried to discipline her and her brother. Her brother moved in with her grandmother when he was a teenager. The life she knew was gone and so was her mother. Things finally settled down when she was fourteen and her mother started dating a man from church. He was nice and crazy about her. They married within a year and life seemed to be back to normal. There wasn't a lot of integration with her father and his wives, as he lived far away.

Advice for parents: Choose who you let into your life wisely. If they do not accept your children with open arms, they do not belong in your life.

Chapter 11

YOURS, MINE, AND OURS

"The light of love sees no walls."
-Suzy Kassem

I felt like I hit the jackpot! Neither Pop nor Veda had been married previously or had children of their own. I know that sounds selfish and it was. I didn't want any more changes going on in my family. Whew! Weren't we enough? There were three of us. Honestly, as a child I recognized that my thoughts were selfish. I shared earlier that my parents were the first to get divorced in my area and among my group of friends. So by time they re-married plenty of people I knew were divorced and re-married. I am telling you it felt like once my parents divorced it was a domino effect. I had already gone through the scary phase of not wanting a step-monster or weird step-father, as friends called them. I had heard the horror stories. Imagine if we had to throw other children in the mix. Nope! Mom was physically unable to have any more children, although she said she would have loved to have a child with Pop. She had a hysterectomy at the age of twenty-seven. Veda did not desire to have children when she married Dad.

There are many blended families when parents get remarried, but for this chapter, the personal experience I will share is when my mom dated a man and he had two children. Oh my goodness, it was so odd. His oldest daughter was my sister's age and his son was my age. They moved to Louisiana from California. I remember Mom and her boyfriend discussing plans for our families. I'd hear him say, "Well, I will have my kids that weekend. What about yours?" Or Mom would say, "No, my kids have games." Comments about, "Mine do not like to do that." "Mine do not eat that." "What do yours like to do?" Try going out to eat and listening to five kids talking about what they are craving! I remember his kids being picky eaters. At our house we didn't go out to eat that often. It was a treat to go on some Fridays and get the Sonic™ brown bag special. Mom would order two of them. Each bag came with two cheeseburgers, two orders of fries or tater tots, and two fountain drinks. We were living the life on those Fridays! I guess this came up more often now because her boyfriend would want to treat us all to dinner at other restaurants.

I suggest saying the children's names instead of "yours, mine, and ours". For example, "Sally and Paul have games at XYZ times on XYZ days. When are Scott and Tricia's games?" Instead of saying, "Our games are XYZ times on XYZ days. When are your kids' games?" There is value in recognizing children by their name and not by "yours, mine, and ours". Children may feel insignificant if they are identified by who they belong to.

We were settled in our life. Our family had our routines. We all knew what each other liked or didn't like. We knew what foods were our favorites and which activities we liked to do. I know this sounds inconsequential, but it wasn't to me. Our family was having to coordinate with their family. This was something new, as this was the first guy my mom introduced us to who had children.

TIP: Strive to discuss plans privately, at least in the

> beginning, for cohesion. Try to avoid saying, "Yours, Mine, and Ours". Children could interpret such as some are more important than others based on who they biologically belong to.

Another hurdle is when you are trying to blend the families and there is a conflict with all of the children's schedules. You are trying to be there for all of them and show support, but you do not want to miss your children's activities or events. Stop right now and think about how you would handle this situation. What would you do or say to the other person's children and to your own? Be prepared to handle these situations and have conversations with all of the children letting them know that each of them are important.

Chapter 12

FORGIVENESS

"Be kind to one another, tenderhearted, forgiving one another; as God in Christ forgave you." -Ephesians 4:32 (ESV)

Merriam-Webster* defines the word forgive as "to cease to feel resentment against an offender." It was difficult to forgive. I will not deny it. Having that weight in my heart felt like the weight of another person on top of me. As I forgave each person, I felt lighter and lighter. During my different phases of forgiveness, it was a great feeling to let go of all the resentment, hurt, anger, and sadness.

I forgave my mom the earliest. I believe I was

fourteen years old at the time. There was not anything in particular she did that I needed to forgive her for, but in general I needed to let go of old hurt feelings and resentment that I held on to. As I looked across my complete family, and thought of how wonderful my life was, I could no longer carry this with me anymore. I let go of some baggage that day. I had everything I ever wanted again, a family, so why would I not let go of the past? It needed to happen, and felt great! I cannot tell you how many times I have asked my mom to forgive me for the hurtful things I said and how I lashed out. It broke my heart that I was that way with family I loved so dear.

One day I was in a mood. I was yelling at her and saying hurtful things to her. I called her a name my dad had used to describe her, and it wasn't a good one. She brought me to her bathroom and washed my mouth out with Irish Spring soap. When I smell Irish Spring soap it brings me to that day. The only day I ever had my mouth cleaned like that! How could she forgive me? Better yet, how could I forgive myself? It embarrasses me to this day to even type these words about that day.

The next person on my list was my dad. Remember earlier when I shared that my dad showed up my senior year in high school to watch me perform at half-time? I had overwhelmingly positive feelings. That night I thought I forgave him. As time passed, I realized that was just a high off of a positive emotion, and I had not forgiven him. The funny thing about forgiveness is that you know deep down whether or not you have forgiven someone. When you are able to share your story without feeling the original hurt you felt during that time of offense, then you are at peace and probably have forgiven the person. Be careful of not letting go of a bad memory specifically because you feel like you have to hold on to it. This could be dangerous to your heart. As time goes on, you feel more and more confident in your forgiveness that you will not have to remember the bad memories. Sharing your testimony and details of your story should be shared in a positive light. If it is negative, then you will be faced with asking yourself, "Have I really forgiven the offender?"

The forgiveness I needed to give my dad was actually for me. It affected me on a daily basis, not him. I only have control of my feelings, emotions, and spiritual well-being, and we can only change the things we control. Tony Robins said, "Forgiveness is a gift you give yourself." I needed to truly forgive him, so I didn't feel so weighed down with my negative feelings.

One night, in the dorm room at college during my junior year, I cried out to God… I mean cried out! I asked him to help me forgive my dad because

I was not able to do this on my own. Soon after this plea and prayer, I truly forgave him and never looked back. This was eleven years after the divorce. I also asked Him that night to convict my heart so I would know when I would need to apologize to someone or forgive someone, because I did not ever want something to have a hold over me like that again. And, I haven't. I finally felt "free." Well, almost.

The last person I needed to forgive was myself. It happened shortly after forgiving my dad. Releasing all of the guilt I felt for how I treated my family during that tough time finally set me completely free from the divorce, the way I acted, the things I said, and disrupting my family. I didn't want to talk about the divorce for a long time and once I let go and forgave myself, I didn't want to talk about it ever again. It was a part of my past that I did not want to reminisce about. If Mom or Dad would bring up different things about the divorce, I would tell them that all of it is in the past. Remember the father/daughter dinner before my wedding? That night, I told Dad that we didn't need to discuss any of it. He apologized for some of his actions and non-actions, and I kept telling him that it was okay. All is forgiven. Turns out, just as I had guilt regarding my actions, he had guilt for his. Even today as an adult, I do not want to hear anymore apologies or stories from the past about the divorce. It's over. That chapter has been closed for a very long time, and in my opinion, does not need to re-open unless we are helping people by sharing our family's story.

Honestly, writing this book has once again confirmed that I am healed from it. My heart has been mended for a long time. This book is not about rehashing the past and bringing up hurt feelings. This book is about telling my story and sharing experiences to help others. There is no other purpose. It is not therapy for me. It is strictly about helping others. As an adult and parent, I realized that my story could help other families. Sharing how I felt as a child going through the divorce, I believe, will encourage parents to consider the tips provided, consider how their children may be feeling, and recognize the gap between adult reasoning and child-like understanding or perception.

> **TIP:** Work with your children to understand forgiveness and what it means for them. There is not a timeframe on when forgiveness comes for the ones who have hurt you or you have hurt. I encourage you to aim for sooner rather than later.

It took Tricia six years to forgive my dad. It was difficult to come to terms with the fact that he was not the man she thought he was. She felt free when she forgave our parents, and their relationships have been able to grow even deeper because of that forgiveness.

Scott forgave Dad approximately twenty-two years after the divorce. He decided to pick up the phone one day and call him. To start off the conversation he said he was sorry for not being a better son and could have tried harder at times. He told Dad he wanted him to be a part of their lives. Dad said he was a good son and apologized for not being a better dad. It took over two decades for Scott to let go of his hurt and feeling as though Dad quit, gave up on him, and didn't want to be his dad.

True forgiveness is not easy. On the contrary, it is probably the toughest of all steps through the divorce process. It cannot be rushed, though. Our minds are filled with many sayings told to us throughout the years, that we almost believe them to be facts now. The one that stands out the most is, "I'll forgive, but I'll never forget." For me, I used to say that with a negative tone. Once I forgave, I could recall memories of what happened, but I do not allow them to have a hold over me. I let go of the negative tone associated with divorce as well. You know what I am talking about. We have all been there. I would say the famous saying, swing my hip out, point my finger, and end it with an exclamation mark! The true test for myself was when I could share my testimony about the divorce or the relationship with my dad, and not have the raw emotions I felt early on.

As I recall certain details, feelings, and situations while writing this book, I do not feel upset or hurt and haven't for years. I have been more concerned about hurting my parents' feelings. I have honestly struggled with whether or not I am articulating what is important enough to share to help parents, because I do not want to hurt anyone's feelings or diminish how far we have come as a family and in our relationships. My intent is genuine. I no longer have that heaviness on my chest since that night of forgiveness.

When hearts are truly healed, there is peace.

* forgive. 2018. In Merriam-Webster.com. Retrieved from https://www.merriam-webster.com/dictionary/forgive

Open MIC Session

Adam didn't have anything to forgive his mom for. He says he has forgiven his dad, but he is honestly not sure at times. He doesn't want to see him. His dad continues to belittle him when he does speak to him. Is that forgivable? He feels it would be a good start for their relationship if he would apologize and own up to what he did, as well as change his behavior of how he continues to treat Adam. All he says is, "Get over it and move on." Adam feels like his dad hates him for telling his mom about the affair, and he hasn't been there for him since that day. There is a barrier between them.

Barbara has never forgiven her father for splitting her and her brother apart. She also has not forgiven her father about the divorce and has no relationship with him. She doesn't believe forgiveness will ever happen. In her eyes, the bridge cannot be mended.

Carrie had always put her mother on a pedestal and she could do no wrong. While defending her mother to her step-mother, she found out in a dramatic way that her mother had an affair in her first marriage. This confrontation happened right after her mom's divorce with her second husband. She was devastated. She cried herself to sleep and truly believes it changed their relationship for many years. Nothing her mother said would justify this in her mind. She came to a point later in life and decided to just get over it. She believes she has forgiven her parents.

Chapter 13

STATISTICS

"Statistics do not speak for themselves."
- Milton Friedman

We have all read statistics about divorce. Sometimes it is helpful to use statistics to get a point across or force the reader to think bigger and in greater detail. However, there are times when I believe it negatively impacts the reader. Statistics can really "drive it home" whether it be in a positive or negative way. For example, when I included the statistic, "Children who come from a home of divorced parents are twice as likely to drop out of high school as their peers who are still living with parents who did not divorce."* in Chapter 2 did you think "Well, this is what I need to prepare for since I am divorced now?" Or did you think, "I will do everything I can for my children not to become a statistic?" Prepare or prevent it?

I encourage you to take every statistic as an alert of what could happen, not what is going to happen. I am a living example of not being a statistic of divorced parents. I graduated from high school. I graduated from college. I made good grades. I did not do drugs. I did not have an eating disorder. I do not have any major psychological problems. I have had a great career in my field. I have been married for twenty-two years and have two children. We have a stable and peaceful home life. I do not have "daddy or mommy issues." I do not have resentment towards religion or Christianity. I do not blame anything on the divorce. The list could go on.

TIP: Do not allow statistics to bring you down. Use them (skewed or not) to fuel the love for yourself and children, as well as motivation to ensure your family does not become a negative statistic.

How are you going to view your life, your children's lives, and the life around you? I believe every statistic and situation brings different vantage points and we interpret them based on how we feel. Are you going to choose to make them positive or negative? Is your glass half full or half empty? I know this sounds simple, but often times as adults we make this complicated. As children we are so innocent and the life around us seems wonderful. We have a child-like faith in all that is good. As we get older our opinions, judgments, and experiences start clouding our views and emotions. Then eventually some of us have a negative outlook on life and everything and everyone around us. I can assure you this is not off topic.

I believe if you choose happiness, love, and positivity during this divorce it will change you, your life, and your children's lives. I am not over exaggerating my words here. You may have a wonderful life right now as you are reading this book. You may already be in a place of happiness, love, and positivity, which is fabulous! If so, let this be a gentle reminder to keep up the positive pace. Do not let yourself go astray during this difficult time and use the divorce as an excuse to give in to negativity, negative statistics, or what you feel is easiest. If you are not in that happy and positive place, and you feel weighed down, discouraged, or in a negative state, rise up to the call of being the best you can be as a person and parent! If you are seeing the negative in every situation or statistic, you must work on changing your vantage point and emotion. Tell yourself out loud and on a daily basis the opposite of what you are telling yourself now.

"Turn lemons into lemonade" comes to mind at the moment. When you bite into a lemon it is extremely sour. It takes work to turn it into lemonade, but you are able to do it. You add a few ingredients to make it sweeter and voilà! You have lemonade. It is sweet versus sour. It is better.

We all get down and out. We are human. What I am encouraging you to do is to take the time to reassess how you feel about everything in general and that will help you identify what your overall attitude is. Is it positive or negative? Is it sweet or sour? In other words, how do you view your life and the life around you? Honestly ask yourself simple questions like:

-When I read a statistic do I prevent it from happening or prepare for it to happen?

-When I drink a glass of tea and the amount goes down, is it half full or half empty?

-Do I believe the people in our world are mostly good or bad?

-Do people do nice things for me because they love me or they feel obligated?

-Did my co-worker or supervisor give me that compliment because he/she appreciated me or does he/she want something from me?

-Are my friends there for me and asking me how I am doing because they care about me or do they just want to know the latest scoop?

When we chose the latter answer on these questions, some might think that makes us a bad person, a sour person, or negative person. In reality, it simply helps to identify how you perceive situations, others' intentions, and life in general. The reason I bring this up is because you have the opportunity to make different choices, which in turn will benefit you and your children. There is no better time to implement this change. Sometimes it takes a life changing event to wipe our eyes free of the fog and clear our minds so we can focus on what is important... love, faith, and family. It is not going to hurt anything or anyone for you to be more positive and less negative; happy and less cynical; sweeter and less sour; and more loving and less guarded.

I am not suggesting you be naïve and believe every day is full of rainbows and unicorns. It goes along the same lines as being prepared, but not paranoid. I am suggesting to you to believe that living our life full of love and happiness does make a difference. Identifying the blessings all around you is more positive than identifying everything that is wrong in your life. Identifying your blessings positively impacts your life, and identifying everything that is wrong in your life will impact your life negatively. Then, at some point, you have not only affected your quality of life, but that of your children. They will typically do what you do. That doesn't mean you will not go through difficult times, but as you go through difficult times you see it as just that, a difficult time that you will get through. You will no longer have an overall mentality of, "This is my life. I cannot ever get a break. My life is bad."

I want to share this unique fact about myself and a notion I have. For a long time (since late college years) I have had this strong pull on my heart about my outlook on life and love in particular. I am loud, a little crazy, and outgoing. People would ask me at parties and still today, "How much have you had to drink?" I would laugh and say, "I've had a lot of H20 or Diet Pepsi, etc." I have a couple of totties every now and then, but generally speaking I am high on life and nothing else. I live each day as positive as I can be, grateful to be alive. It beats the alternative, right? I make the most out of my days, events, and memories created with my family and friends. I do not want to fall asleep each night with any regrets. I live, and I live fully. I believe we choose how to feel towards people and subjects. I chose to feel positive and have a positive attitude and outlook. Will you choose a positive attitude?

As for love, I believe it is the answer to so many

things, situations, and dilemmas. I have a "thing" for hearts. Several years ago, I looked down in a parking lot at a gas station and saw a grease spot in the shape of a heart and thought, "Love IS everywhere." I believe we chose what we want to see. I chose to see love. I have seen so many hearts out of very unique substances: oil, gas, smashed gum, garden hose, rocks, clouds, indentions in concrete, holes in many surfaces, chairs, iron, steel, decorative scrolls, fabric, my blush container, a freckle on my shoulder, sand, wood, and much more. I post them sometimes on Facebook and now I have friends and family who tag me if they see a heart. They'll say, "Vickie, I see love. I see a heart." What will you choose to see? Will you choose love above all things? If you see love and hearts around you, send me your pictures to authorvickiehall@gmail.com. I would love to see them too and share in your joy.

TIP: Choose happiness and love.

When I decided to write this book, I read many articles and statistics about authors and writing. Difficulties were outlined from the length of the process, time and money spent, dealing with rejection, coping with reviews and criticism, etc. I could have let that scare me away from sharing my thoughts and personal story with you. I could have said, "This is too hard. I probably will not get published anyway. Why do it?" Well, that's not how I view things. I am a positive person. I read the information and decided to accept the challenge even though it was difficult. I was not discouraged and negative about this experience. I was encouraged and positive about it. Yes, I was nervous to put myself out there. But I had a choice to make, and I didn't let the information or statistics steer me away from what I felt like I needed to do. I had to ask myself, "What's the worst thing that could happen? A publisher says they are not interested? Okay." For me the worst thing that could have happened would be not to pursue this passion project. This book does not define me. Just like this divorce does not define you.

Our family (all of us) was given grace throughout the divorce and aftermath. There is no doubt about it. We also had parents who were always loving, patient, encouraging, and positive. I couldn't have asked for better parents. I do not know how my life would have ended up if they were negative, guarded, and cynical. I am so appreciative that they were not that way. Make the choice daily to be happy, loving, and positive. It will change your life and your children's lives.

*McLanahan, Sandefur, Growing Up With a Single Parent: What Hurts, What Helps-Harvard University Press, 1994.

Chapter 14

"A CHILD'S INNOCENCE"

"Innocence is like polished armor; it adorns and defends."
- Robert South

Jim and I were married for about three years before we decided to take the plunge and start our family. We talked about it and were so excited to tell our families that we were going to begin trying to get pregnant. I needed to finish that month's birth control pills, and we were off! Off to a new chapter of our lives. Well, so we hoped!

The very next week I received a phone call from my mom. She asked us if she and Pop could come over. We saw them often, but this was different. Her voice did not sound like her usual peppy self. I got an eerie feeling. I didn't know what to think. My parents arrived thirty minutes later. They told us they needed to talk to us and for us to sit down on the sofa. I immediately felt weak and had a flashback to our "famous family meeting" where Mom and Dad were so serious and told us they were separating. The gears in my mind were turning. "Here we go again!" I thought. I just wanted them to spit it out and get it over with! I was getting red and blotchy and felt that bad news was coming. It didn't matter that they didn't fight and loved each other. Mom and Dad had me fooled, so I knew I could be fooled again. In a matter of minutes my thoughts were going places I never thought it would have to go again.

As Mom began to speak, Pop put his hand on her leg. I saw him comforting her. He was not angry, fidgety, or rolling his eyes. Wait a minute! They are not breaking up! What's going on? And then I heard her words, "I have breast cancer." Please don't judge me here, but as her daughter I was so thankful they were not divorcing. I have not shared this with anyone, until now. I was twenty-six years old, and as their child, I could not imagine anything worse than going through another divorce. I was pure in my thoughts and feelings and felt a sense of relief. I know this sounds crazy! I'm sharing these raw emotions and being transparent, because it is meaningful. It did not matter that I was an adult. I am still a child and they are still my parents. That will never change.

Once I realized my worst nightmare was not reoccurring, "adult daughter" kicked in! I said, "Okay. What's the path forward? When is the next appointment? I'm going. When do you think the surgery will be? What's the anticipated treatment plan?" My list of questions continued. I was in the zone and ready to tackle this alongside her and Pop. I had faith that everything would work out. I did not have any doubt. She was a fighter. She was strong. She has her family to support her. As I went on to talk about the level of support we would provide, I nonchalantly said, "Oh, and by the way, Jim and I were going to start trying for a baby, but that is all on hold now. We were going to tell the family next week. Everything happens for a reason, and I am glad you told us now, so all of our focus can be on you and battling cancer."

I had been on Cloud 9 counting down the days until I took my last pill, and all of a sudden it came to a halt. And that was okay. It could wait. In my mind and heart I thought I could handle anything as long as it wasn't another divorce. Let that statement settle with you. As I am typing the simple sentence my heart is pounding. As a child I thought, based on my first experience of divorce, that it would be more difficult to endure it again versus watching my mom battle breast cancer. This is with knowing all of the statistics during that time and how serious cancer is. I was not only confident that I was equipped to deal with Mom having cancer, I was prepared to walk through the storm with her. That is profound. I compared any difficult situation to how I felt after the divorce as a child, and felt if I made it through that I could make it through anything.

Thinking about it now I am grinning at what she said next, "Wait. Wait. Hold up! What did you say?" I repeated it and told her it was fine. Plans can change. Well, that didn't fly with her. The conversation then turned to us starting our family. She was not having it! She did not want us to put having a baby on hold because of her. She explained that having her first grandchild would give her something to look forward to and help her through the surgery, chemotherapy, and radiation. She said she would be very upset if we changed our plans. Now, if you knew my mom you would know that there is no arguing with her. Once her mind is made up, it is made up! My emotions were on a roller coaster that evening.

The following month I got pregnant. I was

ecstatic. Jim was at work, so I went shopping for baby decorations so I could surprise him! I also bought baby items with a card congratulating my parents on being grandparents for the first time. As each day went by I became more and more excited about having a baby. I was grateful for not having morning sickness and feeling great.

One morning when I woke up to get ready for work, I looked down and there was a puddle of blood. I was scared out of my mind that I lost the baby. I felt so weak. My first mommy thoughts were "What have I done or not done that made this happen?" It was after my first trimester and from the way my book I was reading made it sound, miscarriages typically do not happen at this time. It only took a minute for me to snap out of that worry and into being a parent. I called my doctor and we went in for an exam and ultrasound. On the way to the doctor's office I couldn't help but think that my baby did not deserve this. And that's the first time I acknowledged my baby's innocence. The baby didn't ask to be here and didn't have a choice in the matter. He was naïve to everything going on and extremely vulnerable.

Anticipating what the results would be during my visit and if my baby had died, all I could think about was that he was given life and now it may be gone. As the ultrasound technician put the warm gel on my belly and rolled the wand around to see if there was a heartbeat, I held my breath. Why I thought holding my breath would help is beyond me, but I did. When she found the heartbeat I wept and squeezed Jim's hand as tight as possible. I ended up having a complication, but the worst case scenario would be that I may need a C-section if it didn't correct itself. What a relief.

Life was good. Mom healed from her surgery and she was amazing during her chemotherapy treatments. I have never seen anything like it before. She would feel so sick lying on the bathroom floor and would say, "I will not vomit. This will not control me. I will control it." And she never let herself vomit. The nurses at the cancer center were in awe of her strength and spirit. Meanwhile, I had many baby showers and spreadsheets with all of my "to do" lists before the baby arrived. My blood pressure was elevated and being monitored. The swelling was out of control. I had to wear my shoes 1 ½ sizes bigger because each foot looked like a pound of link sausage. I had to cut back on the chips and candy bars! I could no longer wear my wedding ring and bought a band that fit my hot dog looking finger. Reality set in quickly when I called in my blood pressure readings from the weekend one Monday morning.

The nurse put me on hold and my doctor came

on the phone line. She said, "Vickie, please be careful but you need to get to my office ASAP!" I called Jim and he left work to meet me there. I went to check in and the receptionist told me my doctor is expecting me and to go back. I took my urine test, and she came in looking like she was a deer in the headlights. Immediately behind her was the nurse with a wheelchair. She explained my pre-eclampsia had become toxemia. I was told I would be going to assessment at the hospital and would not be leaving until my baby was born and we were well. What? Did I hear her correctly? I was only 34 weeks pregnant. It was not time for him to be here yet. My book says he has more developing and growing to do. I am not done with my thank you notes. The car seat is not in our vehicle. His clothes are not washed in the special detergent. I still had returns to make at the baby store. The nursery was not ready. I had so many tests and then an ultrasound.

Why am I going through this lengthy story? How does this affect you and what you are going through? Everyone loves to tell the story of when their baby was born, right? Unfortunately, at that point I did not know what was going to happen and if my baby was okay. As much as we planned and tried to prepare for his arrival, we were still not prepared. I want you to bring yourself back to the days and months when you were going through the forty weeks of pregnancy as a parent. You would do anything to protect your child. You wanted what was best for him/her. Both your level of excitement and fear were through the roof. The excitement was for the new life you were bringing into the world and the beginning of your family. The fear was sometimes overwhelming, but was a reality of the world he/she would live in. Why did we have those emotions as parents? The answer is the innocence of a child. We have the joy as parents to witness their purity and disappointment that we are unable to protect them from losing it. As our children get older and experience life it becomes more and more difficult to protect them, but we try. The Tooth Fairy, Easter Bunny, and Santa Claus come to my mind. The longer my children believed, the more innocent I thought they were. As soon as they no longer believed, the sooner I had to realize they were growing up and making their own decisions. Their innocent and unquestionable trust they had in every word I said was gone.

Once my doctor came in and told us the baby was fine and fully developed I was reassured. In my world all was good. In my world, if he was fine I was fine. Everything she said about me and my risks fell on deaf ears. It didn't matter. His life was more important than mine. I looked horrible, felt horrible, and thought I was going to pop! A week later I was induced and 17 ½ hours later my first son was born by a C-section. Everything I went through was worth it, as you know being a parent yourself. When I saw him for the first time nothing else mattered. The world was still spinning around me, but time stopped for me. I remember it like yesterday. My memory is vivid and I pray it remains with me for a lifetime. He was precious. He was a gift entrusted to us. He was so innocent.

As I write this chapter emotions come over me that are difficult to express with words. I want you to now think of that day or a similar moment with your child. Pause, take a deep breath, and reflect on the time you recognized your child's innocence and what you would do to protect it. What were your initial feelings? What came over you? Now, fast forward to today. Are your feelings the same? Do you think this divorce changed your feelings? Would you still do anything to protect the innocence of your child? I believe your answer is "yes". Regardless of your child's age, he/she will always have the innocent and pure expectation of you, and you will always want to protect them. A child's innocence with regards to their parents should remain the same. The only way a child's expectation changes is if a parent changes.

TIP: Do not allow this divorce to affect you in a way that risks your child's innocence of who you are and what you would do for them.

After I became a parent I had a different level of emotions as I looked back in time at my parents' divorce and life that followed. I realized how difficult it was to be a parent. Being a parent is the most stressful job a person can have. There is nothing that can fully prepare you for a parent's "job description". You take things as they come. You do your best in the moment. You hope and pray that your best is good enough. You buckle up, ride the roller coaster, hold on tight, close your eyes, and hope you and your children make it to the end of the ride. I get it. Trust me. I get it. The flip side of being a parent and looking back is that I cannot justify why a parent would allow a divorce with a past love to affect the relationship with his/her children. Nothing comes to mind where that scenario is acceptable. **There should be no excuses when it comes to your children.** They are innocent, blameless, and do not deserve anything but your best. I honestly cannot cut you any slack, as I hold myself to the same standard. When I feel like I could have done better or said something different I learn from it and make the adjustment going forward. Do not beat yourself up on what you may have said or done wrong in the past. Do not look back, look forward. You cannot change the past. You can, however, make better choices now and in the future. All of this is worth it to me because I love my sons and treasure our relationships. There is not a limit on the amount of sacrifice I would endure for my children. I personally relate this to the level of sacrifice He has endured for us, his children. Do not pity yourself for having to deal with this divorce. Be grateful for your children. They did not ask to be here. You chose for them to be here. You wanted your children. Show them you still want them in your life by your words and actions. If you don't they will assume they no longer matter to you.

Chapter 15

COMMUNICATION IS CRUCIAL

"The single biggest problem in communication is the illusion that it has taken place." - George Bernard Shaw

In today's society, and even as far back as my college years, communication was pushed heavily in all aspects of my life: school, personal, work, relationships of any kind, and spiritually. I would hear or read "Communication is key in any relationship."; "Communication is the most important aspect to understanding expectations."; "Communicating with God is important."; "Have open communication with your children.";

"Communication is the key to success."; "Communication is the key to teamwork." The list goes on. It is as though communication is the key to unlocking every door around me. It has now been engrained in me. I have learned to understand the importance of it and just how much weight it holds in any situation.

In college, I talked about everything with my friends, and I mean everything. We would sit in groups and share our stories with each other. We could say what was on our minds and because we all knew the intentions were good, our feelings did not get hurt. We did not judge each other and think poorly of one another because of our choices, whether they were good or bad; right or wrong. We learned with maturity that knowing other people who are not just like us was a positive thing and should be embraced. I grew as a person by communicating with others and listening to their stories. It expanded my thought process, how I treated others, and responded in dialogue.

A dear friend of mine came to me with a serious look on her face during our sophomore year of college. I didn't know what was wrong with her and then she started to speak. I listened intently. She had decided to leave school. She was pregnant. She began to share her story about who this guy was, how she knew him, and what happened. She went home for a funeral and ran into him. He was an old friend. He was there for her and one thing led to another. She was not sure what to do about it and asked me what I thought about all of this and my opinions on adoption and abortion. She then proceeded to tell me that there was one more concern. The guy was of a different race. So on top of her trying to figure out what she needed to do with her baby, she was wondering how she was not only going to tell her parents she was pregnant, but that her baby would be biracial. There were lots of tears and emotions. My heart was breaking for her. I was so glad she felt comfortable enough to come to me and I contemplated with what to say. How I responded in that moment could possibly affect her actions going forward.

I listened to my dear friend and was there for her. She looked at me with her eyes filled with tears and said, "So what do you think? What would you do?" Do any of us truly know what we would actually do until we are in a situation? I took a deep breath. I let her know I would be there for her no matter what she decided, and told her that her parents would love her regardless and so would I. I recommended she research the options, speak with her parents, and pray about it. I told her that she was the one who was going to live with the decision, so she had to be the one to make it. I prayed for her non-stop. After all was said and done, she went through a Christian adoption organization and received counseling throughout her entire pregnancy. Her baby was adopted by a family who was excited to grow their family, and who were unable to have children of their own biologically. In communicating with someone, we are not only listening, we are talking. Anytime we speak words we are to be mindful of how those words could impact someone. This is the case in any relationship. Our words influence others. We are to be responsible for effectively communicating our feelings, but also responsible for how we communicate them. This includes body language too. My mom used to say, "It is not always what you say, it is how you say it."

What would she have done had I responded differently? None of us know that answer. But in that moment I had to decide on what I should say. I was not her parent. I was her friend. I was hesitant to tell her what to do specifically, because I am not the one that would have to live with the consequences either way. We should do our best to use discernment when communicating with others. Be sensitive to what the person is saying and how they are feeling.

Communication was a hot topic in school as

well. My college professors expressed time and time again not to wait until something got so bad with our class or understanding of material to come see them. We were to go see them as soon as we had a question and/or concern. That was when I first heard of an "Open Door Policy". They wanted us to feel comfortable and to know that their door was always open to students. We just needed to walk right in to meet with them. That sounds easier to do than what is was. We were a little intimidated by our college professors. Even though I attended a small college they were our teachers and we were their students. It took some getting used to. Once I felt that my professors really cared and meant what they said, and it wasn't just another policy, I did go speak with them and take advantage of having that access.

This leads me to the professional workplace. There are so many communication techniques and trainings for supervisors, leaders, and employees to use and learn about. The "Open Door Policy" continued to be a big hit here also. The Human Resources Department and managers wanted everyone to know that their door was always open and it was a safe place to speak freely and confidentially. Almost every job posting wants candidates who communicate effectively with others and at all levels. Well of course they do! People need to be able to work with each other, get along, and communicate. That is part of working. It is a must that we are able to communicate in order to get our jobs done and have cohesion.

In books, articles, motivational speeches, and podcasts the big rave is about how important communication is with all relationships. This is with any relationship: boyfriend, spouse, friend, child, parent, co-worker, God, and every other role you can think of, and I get it. I think it is fabulous. We have all heard the sayings to remind us about improving our communication skills. "Think before you speak." "Before you talk, listen." "Talk to God just like you are speaking with a friend."

With our children we have reiterated over and over again to communicate with us and that we will answer any question they have. We have told them they will not be in trouble for talking to us and asking questions. We have also told them that they can tell us anything about themselves and their friends without judgment. We call it our family circle of trust. As long as what they are telling us does not put them or their friends in danger and put someone else in danger we will not tell their parents. Meaning, unless it is something truly detrimental we will not share it. There have been times where I had to share the information, because the child was at risk of hurting themselves or someone else.

As I think back to my childhood, and through high school, I never felt as though I was missing out on anything with my parents, siblings, and other family members. Yet, it was a different time in comparison to the last twenty years. We did not talk about everything. As a young lady it was not proper to discuss certain topics in front of mixed company, or at all. I felt like my mom knew everything that she needed to know, and I was open to the degree that I thought was acceptable at the time. We were close enough that if I truly had serious questions I think I would have asked, but we didn't sit around and discuss every detail of our day, how we were feeling and what was going on with us and our friends. We would share in general how our day went at school, but not in depth conversations.

As a young girl I was too embarrassed to talk to my mom about my menstrual cycle. I remember my sister saying it was going to happen and to let her know if I had any questions. They taught us about it in our Physical Education class at school. It was a short video and of course we were all disgusted. I told my mom about it once it started, but I didn't understand what was going on with my body and why I was having it. I didn't know what to expect other than what I learned at school and what my sister shared with her experiences, which wasn't very much.

Do not even think of talking about sex in our household. Oh my! It was not discussed. I was told and taught to just not do it until I was married.

After Mom married Pop, I would feel guilty sometimes about hurting over my dad or still thinking about the divorce. I didn't want to hurt them by talking too much about it. It continued to feel like a broken record. When I did talk about the divorce or my feelings, it was the same thing over and over again.

As I got older, I remember my dad saying, "You know you can talk to me about the divorce if you need to." I would just shrug it off. Our time together was not extensive so I didn't want to spend it crying and being upset in a deep conversation. Nothing was going to change the past so why talk about it?

One of my regrets, once I began learning how significant communication was, was not opening up to my dad sooner. Sometimes I think if I had talked to him more about it maybe our relationship would have ended up being better sooner. I know it is hindsight now. I am sharing this because it is extremely important to communicate openly. Communication is an element of a relationship that makes a huge difference between the two people. I cannot go back in time, none of us can, but if I could this is one thing I would have changed.

TIP: You cannot force your children to communicate with you. You can, however, constantly reinforce to them that they can tell you anything (along with any parameters you feel necessary) and ensure they feel safe to do so.

I was conflicted with the fact that as I was learning so much about communication in college, I was also at the cusp of forgiving my dad. I was scared. Once I forgave him I didn't really want to talk about the divorce and my feelings. It controlled me for so long that I didn't want it to be the topic of our conversations. I didn't want to waste any more of my breath and feelings on it. I wanted to put it all behind me at that point. I have learned that once I forgive someone it is still okay to speak about it, share the feelings associated with it, and share testimony as long as it isn't out of malice. It should be for growth and helping people who have gone through or are going through a similar situation.

Time passed by. My dad retired early from his chemical plant job, and went to college to become a Pastor. I was happy for him for going back to college. I went to his graduation. My Maw Maw Mary was there and she was all smiles seeing him walk across the stage and so was I. It was a huge accomplishment. He then became an Associate Pastor at the church he was attending. When I got engaged to Jim I was over the moon and couldn't wait to get married. We had the venue booked the next day. My mom and I met with the wedding planner and I brought home samples of invitations and napkins. I found my dress quickly. The flowers were ordered and the photographer was booked. You name it, it was done. Showers were scheduled. The registry was done. Engagement pictures and formal pictures were scheduled. We didn't get stressed out about the logistics or anything. I was not one of the brides-to-be that lost weight and couldn't eat because of stress. My dress had to be let out another ½ inch at my last fitting. The only stress I felt was deciding how to ensure both sets of parents felt included, specifically my dad and Veda. I did not want anyone getting hurt. Our invitations would need to list all parents; the engagement and wedding announcements needed the same; all of them needed to be seated on the first row; how would I be escorted? What about the father/daughter dance? I took everyone and everything into account for my wedding day.

I decided to walk down the staircase; Pop would meet me at the bottom of the staircase and escort me to the back of the middle aisle. Dad would join us and they would both escort me down the aisle and present me to Jim. It was perfect. I had my special time with Pop and then both of them. For the father/daughter dance I asked each of them to dance with me. We would have our dances separately. I would dance with Pop for one song and with Dad on the next song. I wasn't expecting the answer I received from my dad... or the hurt.

Dad told me that this very issue recently got brought up in their church over a man, one of the leaders in the church, who danced with his daughter at her wedding. He said it wasn't a good situation and there was drama over it. He went on further to say that he wasn't going to dance with me because the church would frown upon it. I kept it together and told him I understood. Why did I say that? Why did I say I understood? I did not understand. I have gone out of my way to ensure he and Veda were included in everything and wanted to make sure they were just as much a part of this wedding as Mom and Pop. I was only getting married once. I wanted to have our dance together. The 2 ½ minutes may not have meant anything to him, but it did to me. I was twenty-five years old, but I was still his child. Why couldn't I say these things to him? Why couldn't I be honest about my feelings? I sucked it up. I cried to Mom and Pop and had to get over it. I have never shared this with him, because I did get over it. I didn't want to talk about it ever again. As I recall this from twenty years ago, I still wonder why I couldn't just tell him how I felt. I am not a person who yells and screams and carries on. I definitely would not have done that. Children should be able to tell their parents anything. Why not just say how I felt at the time? It probably wouldn't have changed his decision, but I would have felt better and maybe could have understood where he was coming from if it was discussed. The reason I believe I did not talk to him was because I was not comfortable enough to. At that time we didn't have open communication per se, and I did not want to come across as petty and selfish.

Earlier in the book I mentioned that my sister was struggling with taking her own life in high school. She wrote my mom a letter and left it in her room to read. My mom and sister talked, and changes were made. I am so grateful my sister had the courage to share her feelings and that my mom was there for her to help her through such a difficult time. I didn't find this out until years after it happened. I think about my sister and cannot imagine what she was going through and how it impacted her. We shared a bedroom, and I didn't know how she was feeling. What I finally had to realize was that she didn't tell me, but she told someone... my mom. That is what is key here. She communicated when she needed to and it unlocked the door to working through her feelings.

We can all learn from our own stories and stories from others, including Tricia's story. We need to communicate with each other in all roles, and children need to have comfort in knowing they can speak to their parents about anything. This is a must. When it came right down to the serious stuff Tricia was able to share her feelings with Mom.

I am hurting as I write this chapter. Typing this section about my son is affecting me more than I thought it would. I feel I need to be transparent. I got to this point in the chapter and was going to drive it home on closing sentences of how important communication is and it going both ways. Parent to child, and child to parent. Part of me feels like the following is not my story to share, it is my son's. The other part of me is drawn to share this with you as a parent in hopes that you too will be on the bandwagon with communication and how very important and significant it is. This all has been recent so please bear with me. Well, what am I thinking? When you read this you won't hear the pause in my voice and see me cry. I apologize. I will get on with it. My son did say it was acceptable to him for me to share this with you.

About a year-and-a-half ago, I was talking with my son and it was another good and long conversation. He started fidgeting and looking down. I asked him, "What is wrong?" "You can tell momma anything." He began to weep and started blurting out all of these deep feelings. I could not believe what I was hearing. I could not believe my son was hurting as much as he was, and he thought possibly our life could be better without him. How could he think the world may be better if he wasn't in it? He and his brother are our world. There are not enough words I can use to express my feelings and emotions as I listened to his hurt and saw him break down. He went on to explain that he did not know what his purpose was in life. He told me that he did not think about hurting himself or taking his own life, but was having so many different thoughts running through his mind. He was down. At the time he was fourteen.

As a parent I was thankful and relieved he came to me and communicated his thoughts and feelings. It was difficult to hear and keep it together, but I did. We got him the help he needed and told him that we wanted him to be happy, health, and whole. We reinforced that we would be there for him every step of the way as he worked through things. I was a teenager once and remember things I went through and how I felt. This seemed like more than everyday teenager stuff. At his age, he was wondering what his purpose in life was and how it fit in with the big picture. I was nowhere near those questions at his age. There is access to so much information now on the internet. Children's brains get overloaded with all that they read and hear. Throw that on top of being a teenager with hormones, peer pressure, friend drama, school drama, and family dynamics, they are quickly overwhelmed and questioning a lot of things around them.

What would have happened had he not come to talk to me? How much longer would he have gone feeling that way with no help and direction? It is one of the most painful and scary times I have been through as a parent. The important point is that he did communicate. He did feel safe with us as his parents.

Communication is crucial. It is also crucial that your children feel comfortable enough to communicate with you and feel protected. Children want to feel safe with their parents; safe to speak and share without judgment, safe from harm and danger, safe to be themselves, protected and shielded in the general sense. Your children will get their information from somewhere. Your children will get their comfort from someone. Make sure it is from you!

Parents are equivalent to life jackets. When a person jumps in the water with a life jacket on he/she will float to the top. Sure, the person may move up and down and side to side like a cork, but he/she will remain at the top of the water. What happens when the person is not wearing a life jacket? The person sinks to the bottom where the water is deep and there is unknown territory. When the person swims up to the top he/she wants to be thrown a life jacket to save them! That is if the person can swim. What if it is an infant, toddler, or older person who cannot swim? Would you allow him/her to jump into the water without the life jacket? No, I do not believe you would. You would protect the person and put the life jacket on him/her first to prevent them from drowning.

Be your children's life jacket in this ocean of life. That is what they expect from you. They are treading water and need a life jacket. Save them! Make sure they know they are not going through this alone. Keep reinforcing communication and that you are there to listen anytime they need to talk.

Open MIC Session

Adam doesn't feel like he can communicate with his dad at all, so the likelihood that they would be on the same page is slim. He does not understand his dad and his dad does not understand him. When they did try to communicate their perceptions and understanding of each other were never aligned.

Barbara does not have anything to add that is new. There was never communication after the divorce. Her perception of his lack of words and actions is the same as their reality. Communication was non-existent.

Carrie didn't have a lot of communication when she was younger. She had a tremendous amount of responsibility put on her and they didn't talk it out often.

Chapter 16

FINANCIAL SUPPORT

"Time is more valuable than money. You can get more money, but you cannot get more time." - Jim Rohn

This subject was going to get addressed at some point, so here goes. I have it as a latter chapter, because I didn't want you to get uncomfortable or fidgety in the beginning of my story. No one ever really enjoys talking about money, child support, or their financial obligations, yet the topic gets discussed often. I have heard parents arguing about child support and/or questioning the amount of child support and it has been negative in nature.

Just in what I have witnessed there have been more arguments about money than how much time is spent with the children. I am not saying the parents are more concerned about money than their children, but that is what they are choosing to complain or argue about the most. Why is that? Is it that a parent is so bitter they cannot stand to write the check to the other one? Is it that a parent didn't realize how much it actually cost to raise a child or how expensive everything is?

Each time parents discuss expanding their family the topic of the expenses associated with having another child is brought up in the conversation, and it needs to be. My husband and I talked about this as well. It is a responsible approach to confirm you are able to take care of your children financially. That is part of being a parent. We discussed everything else that went along with it, but money was definitely part of the formula in making our decision.

Kathryn Vasel of CNN Money (New York) published an article on January 9, 2017; *It costs $233,610 to raise a child.* The article is eye-catching and pocket-catching. "A middle-income, married couple with two children is estimated to spend $233,610 to raise a child born in 2015, according to a report released by the Department of Agriculture Monday. That number only covers costs from birth through age 17-- so it doesn't include college expenses." It sounds like a lot of money, and it is, but as I read the article on the surface I thought, "Wait, does that include if the child goes to private school, drives a car, is involved in extracurricular activities, goes on family vacations, receives allowance, etc.?" As a parent those are just a few things that came to mind. I also noticed the article continued to reference "married-couple households". Does that mean it is more expensive if the parents are single or divorced? The article goes on further to say that "Married-couple households that had three or more children spent 24% less on average per child compared to those with two kids. As families increase in size, children may share a bedroom, clothing and toys can be reused, and food can be purchased in larger, more economical packages."

If I use the figure $233,610 (average expense to raise a child) and divide it by 17 (their age) and divide it by 2 (number of parents), I get $6,870.88, which is $572.57 per child per month. This is only hypothetical in nature and is based on the article and its source from three years ago. When child support is calculated other factors may be included, because as I mentioned, I am uncertain of everything that is included in this number above of how much it costs to raise a child. We know for certain it is only until the age of 17. Most high school graduates are 18; then there are college expenses, which were not included.

Google defines the noun "child support" as *court-ordered payments, typically made by a noncustodial divorced parent, to support one's minor child or children.*

According to the latest version of the government's *Custodial Mothers and Fathers and Their Child Support report*, which was released in January 2016, there are currently 13.4 million custodial single parents living in the United States and about half of them (48.7%) have some type of legal or informal child support agreement in place. On average, custodial single parents who receive child support get about $329 per month to help with food, shelter, clothing, medical costs, education, and incidentals.*

When I was growing up my dad paid child support and paid on time…and he didn't hesitate to tell us either. He would say, "You know only 50% of dads pay child support, and I pay it. I pay it every month on time to your mother." I didn't understand why he was telling me this information. What do I say? Thank you? It felt very awkward.

> **TIP:** Child support does not need to be discussed with your children. It is a legal obligation and an adult topic of discussion.

There were times when my dad would pay for certain things outside of child support. He used to give Mom extra money for school clothes and supplies. I remember when I started taking piano lessons, and he helped buy my piano and pay for the lessons. When I was in high school he bought me an open-hole flute. I was ecstatic! I had a nickel plated flute since fifth grade, so this was a huge upgrade. When I went to college he gave me $1,000 per semester. I was thankful for his financial support in my life.

Money has always been and will continue to be a sensitive subject. I get it. Children do not want to be a burden to their parents. They also expect things to be the same as they were before the divorce in this area. If there are going to be changes in the financial situation which are significant I suggest explaining it to them on their level. I wouldn't recommend you say things like, "I give your mom/dad money for that. Ask her/him for it." Or "I give your mom/dad child support and this is included." Children are going to ask you for things just as they did before, whether it is for candy, school trips, extra dance lessons, clothes, spending money, etc.

TIP: Communicate with the other parent on what the responses should be, just as you did

> when you were married, especially on big purchases. Ensure alignment on what you both feel the children should have or shouldn't have.

Be mindful that your children's expectations of you have not changed now that you are divorced. They will remain the same, if not higher. If you are unable to pay for something or simply do not want him/her to have an item, then let the child know just as you would have done before the divorce. For example, if you are out shopping with your daughter and she wants a pair of shorts, decide if you want to buy them or not based on what you feel is best for her at that time and your budget. If the answer is no it should be no because she doesn't need them right now or it is not budgeted, not because clothes are included as an expense in child support. A response could be, "We are buying you clothes for summertime next month. You will be able to pick out all kinds of shorts and tops then." Another example is if your son asks you if you would pay for an upcoming school trip. How would you have handled it before the divorce? Would you make the decision on your own or speak to your spouse before responding? I would suggest telling him that you will need to speak with his mom/dad. You may even ask, "Have you already asked your mom/dad?" As we know, sometimes a child already received an answer from one of the parents, but it wasn't the answer the child wanted, so he/she asks the other parent. That happens regardless of whether or not the parents are divorced. When you are in the grocery store and your children ask for candy. Either let them have the candy or not, but please do not say, "I do not have the money for extras since your mother/father and I divorced." As you hear these examples, pause for a minute and recognize the difference in the responses. The word divorce or your mother/father are not needed to justify your answer to your children.

I understand times may be frustrating when it comes to money. It could be that before the divorce you could pay for items whenever you wanted to, but now that has changed. You may know that and I may know that, but your children do not need to know it. Your children do not need to know the details of any financial limitations or have them associated with the divorce. Saying, "It is not in our budget this month." is completely different than "You know we cannot afford this now that your mother/father and I are no longer together." The last thing you want to have happen is for your children to feel as though this is another hurdle because of the divorce. As parents, it is okay if we do not purchase everything right then as the children ask for it, budgeted or not. Find ways to express your response without connecting the reason to the divorce or other parent.

* United States. Census Department. Custodial Mothers and Fathers and Their Child Support: 2013. By Timothy Grall. U.S. Census, January 2016. [https://www.census.gov/content/dam/Census/library/publications/2016/demo/P60-255.pdf].

Chapter 17

PERCEPTIONS

""Most disagreements are caused by different perceptions that created different realities." - thebeststatusmessages.com

We can read the same book and take away a different message. We can listen to the same conversation and hear a different story. We can look at the same picture and perceive it differently.

Take a moment to look at the images on the next page. What do you see? If we take a moment and think about perpective, we can understand better how to communicate with others.

Is the glass half empty or half full?

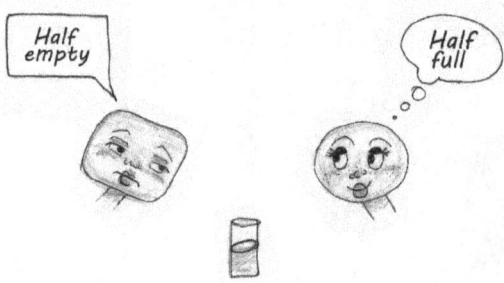

Do you see four or three sticks?

Is it the letter M or W?

The main purpose of this book is to help parents identify that there is a gap between adult reasoning and the children's perceptions. In our minds as parents we are justified in what we are saying and doing, our words and actions. Parents would not say or do them if they thought otherwise. With that being said please recognize that your children do not always see, hear, and understand words and actions the same way you do. As that becomes clearer to you adjustments may be made in hopes to reduce the gap of understanding and in turn help make this divorce better.

Let's review examples in the table below:

PARENTS SAYS	CHILD HEARS
This is not your fault.	Could this be my fault?
We fell out of love.	Can they fall out of love with me?
I cannot see you. I have _____ this weekend.	I am not as important as _____. I am not important.
That is included in the child support I pay each month.	Am I a burden? I am a burden.
I am not picking you up since your other siblings aren't coming.	I am not worth his/her time. I am not enough. I am rejected.
Sorry I didn't call. I lost track of time. Was busy.	I do not matter. I am not worth it.
Cancellations	Broken Promises
Consecutive no-shows	He/She has forgotten about me.

My brother, Scott, shared a perception that was very impactful and relevant. The first time my dad said, "Son, I am not coming to pick you up this weekend since the girls aren't coming," he felt that was the day Dad gave up. He quit. The time spent together was not worth it to him. Scott was not worth it. When you hear this, what do you think? Do you think my dad said that because he felt the way Scott did? See how one sentence, one perception can change the way a child feels?

> **TIP:** Do your best to confirm your children understand your words and actions. For example, you could ask, "Did you understand what I meant when I said XYZ? It seems as though you are upset. Let's talk more about it." Or "Do you understand why I couldn't be there or XYZ?"

Parenting is hard. I cannot imagine parenting after a divorce because you are trying to process your feelings and your children's feelings. With everything that comes along with a divorce and being in separate households it seems even more challenging. No matter how hard it gets, do not quit fighting for your children's attention, time, and love. They are worth it. They are a part of you. When communicating if you hear a crack in their voice, notice their body language changes, they look away, or fidget, ask them what is wrong. Ask them if you said something that hurt them. Explain that you love them and you do not ever want to hurt them or have them feel rejected. For more on communication see chapter 15.

I recently listened to a dear friend share her feelings about a sensitive subject. I believe this story is another good illustration of how a child, regardless of their age, perceives a parent's actions differently than how parents do. Her parents divorced fourteen years ago when she was an adult at thirty years old. Both parents have been re-married for years. Her dad and his wife were married abroad at an all-inclusive resort. Her step-mom approached her about writing a letter in support of her dad's and mom's marriage being annulled. Once this was all approved, they could then be married in a Catholic church. As I sat in the room and looked around me I was the only non-Catholic person listening. I didn't feel uncomfortable, as I wasn't there to state my opinion from a religious perspective. I was there to listen to a friend talk about how it felt being his child and asked to do this.

My friend was outraged that her step-mom would ask her that. Her dad walked in from outside in the middle of the discussion and asked what was being talked about, as he could see the look of shock on his daughter's face. She told him and he said, "Will you do this for me? We want to get married in the Catholic Church." She said, "No", and he asked again while placing his hand on her shoulder, "I'll ask you again. Will you do this for me?" She stayed firm with her response. She also let him know that she couldn't believe the audacity of this request, much less that it didn't come from him.

From her perspective as a child, she feels as though this would support erasing her parent's history, her family's history and that she and her siblings would be considered bastards in the eyes of the church. She also does not agree with it being necessary, as they are already married. She continued to share that she doesn't understand why it is so important now to him. He didn't go to church when they were growing up, and it wasn't important to him then. She was also offended that her step-mom called her a non-Catholic, when she was confirmed in the Catholic Church at the age of seventeen. There were a lot of feelings shared that night, and I could see the hurt in her eyes, because she didn't agree with it, she didn't see the need to do it. She thought asking a child to be involved with answering questions and writing a letter about her parents' marriage was unacceptable and selfish.

This is not a religious issue, nor do I want it

to turn in to one. I read an article, *12 Myths About Marriage Annulments in the Catholic Church**. "An annulment in the Catholic Church deals only with the sacrament of marriage, and not the legal, historical, emotional truth of marriage. An annulment states that the sacrament was never present, and not that the marriage never took place. An annulment looks at marriage from the perspective of the Gospel and of Church doctrine. An annulment has no effect at all on the legitimacy of children."* Once six letters and questionnaires are submitted and the annulment goes through the process, the Tribunal (Court of Law for the Church) sends the judgment on whether or not the marriage will be annulled. It was interesting to read. Some of the reasons why my friend didn't want to write the letter and support the annulment are considered myths. However, reading truths versus myths doesn't negate how she was feeling as her dad's daughter. She would have to agree that the sacrament of marriage was never present in her parents' marriage. Wasn't it though in the beginning? Is this fair to ask of a child?

As you read her story, what do you think? Is she justified in saying no to her dad? Do you think he understands why she doesn't want to write the letter? Do you think she understands why it is so important to him for her to do it and support his request? Have you experienced a similar situation with your children? What would you say or do to clear it up?

If someone's perception is not the same as your perception it doesn't mean they are right or wrong, it is different. Understanding your children's feelings and their perceptions will make a difference as your family deals with this divorce.

*12 Myths About Marriage Annulments in the Catholic Church, The Diocese of Harrisburg, Pennsylvania, https://www.hbgdiocese.org/tribunal/divorce-and-remarriage/12-myths-about-marriage-annulments/

Chapter 18

YOUR CHILDREN'S RELATIONSHIPS

""I want the kind of marriage that makes my kids want to get married." - Emily Wierenga

My grandparents were divorced. My parents were divorced. I did not want to be divorced. It sounds silly as I type it. I do not believe anyone wants to be divorced. When I was growing up I didn't envision having a big wedding with lots of flowers, a twenty foot train, ten bridesmaids, hundreds of wedding presents, guests throwing rice, and driving away in the sunset. We have all seen the commercials and movies that have the bride and groom drive off and look out of the back window smiling and waving, while the cans are dinging against the asphalt. I dreamed of marrying a man, having children, living life, smiling, growing old together, having grandchildren, and dying together like the sweet old couple did on the movie, Titanic. I am not kidding. When I saw the movie I thought it was one of the sweetest scenes I had ever watched. The old couple lived and built their life together, were traveling across the world on a ship, making memories, and as the water was rising in the ship they lied on the bed holding hands looking at each other as the water line filled above them.

I wanted what my grandparents (Granny and Pappy) had. I wanted what my parents had once they re-married. As I got older, I began to understand more about marriage. Not only would I pray for God to send me the man He had in store for me when He was ready, I also began developing an image in my mind of what kind of man I wanted. I didn't have a tangible list per se, but I did expect my husband to have certain characteristics, morals, and beliefs. Without even realizing it I was drawing these expectations off of what was present in my own life. I had three beautiful couples inside and out who influenced me.

In life, it is human nature to either want what you know and are familiar with because you had a positive connection to it, or you want completely opposite of what you know because you had a negative connection to it. For me, I had positive connections to witnessing my grandparents' and parents' marriages. That is what I wanted for my marriage.

For example, my mom grew up with five siblings. Her father left my grandmother and the children. My grandmother had not worked outside of the home at that point and now it was necessary to get a job. She was devastated about her husband leaving and the children not having a father. They were poor, alone, and had to take care of each other. She felt as though her mom was never home. Some nights they were lucky to find something to eat and the living conditions were not good. When I close my eyes and think of six children trying to survive on their own, I cringe. Starting with the oldest child they each did what they could to be there for one another. As an adult I try to be positive and think that my grandmother did the best she could with what she knew in the 1960s with six children. As a child I could not imagine a life such as my mom's childhood. Maw Maw Pat was not the mother my mom desired to be once she had children. Mom promised herself that she would be everything her mother wasn't to Tricia, me, and Scott. She had a negative connection to the experience of growing up with a mom such as hers at that time of her life. Therefore, she wanted to be to her children what she desired as a child; the opposite of what she had present in her life. I could not ask for a better mom.

I had a positive connection to growing up with the mom I had in my life. She represented everything I wanted to be as a mom to my children.

My husband's parents were divorced. After a certain length of time, his dad was no longer in the picture. He was a great father before the divorce and shortly after, and then it changed dramatically after a weekend visit. During a drop off on a sunny Sunday afternoon Jim's dad was saying his good-byes to his sisters. As Jim went to get out of the car his dad said, "Jim, I won't be seeing y'all as much anymore, I need to spend more time with my girlfriend." Jim said some choice words and slammed the car door. Picture being in sixth grade and one of your parents telling you someone else is more important than you are in their life. Jim walked away and has never looked back, and neither has his dad. He told himself if he was ever a dad he would be everything his dad wasn't to him. This was also due to his negative connection to that experience. Our boys have the absolute best dad ever! I hope they take their positive connections to their experiences and are the same and better for their children.

TIP: Make a daily choice to be your best in all that you do! Focus on the positive in all things.

Not everyone has the above revelation and unfortunately some people continue a pattern or behavior because that is all they know and it is too difficult to learn another way regardless of whether they had a negative connection to it or not. One night, a dear friend showed up at our door with her one year old child. My friend's face was bruised and there were marks on her skin. Her husband had physically abused her. We got the baby settled in and put to bed, as it was late at night. She began to share her story and I will say it shocked me. Her husband seemed so nice and friendly. He portrayed to all of us that he loved and adored her. Part of her story was sharing his childhood story. His dad used to abuse him. His dad didn't know how to deal with and manage his anger when he was growing up, so he thought that was the way I guess. The next day, we got her into a woman's shelter. She eventually went home. They went through counseling and things seemed to have gotten better. Time would pass and it would happen again, again, and again. At one point I remember meeting her at a restaurant parking lot and she said she was finally going to leave. I had heard this before. Needless to say it didn't happen. Things didn't change and regardless of how many days or months there were in between beatings, it continued to happen. Fast forward twenty years and they are still together, and he manages his anger the same way his father did when he was a child.

It saddens me when this transpires and people with negative connections to experiences continue the same behavior they despised as a child. I believe people can be who they want to be and who God designed them to be. I am not saying it is not hard to go against the grain of what people are familiar with. My hope for everyone, especially parents, is to be better. Be better than what you do know. Be better than what you do not know.

This leads into my sister's story. Tricia was the oldest child. You remember some of her experiences shared earlier in the book. Tricia met her husband, dated, fell in love, married, and moved out of state. About six months into her marriage she called upset asking, "What have I done?" She said she wanted to get in her little red car and drive home. She was thirteen hours way. She talked and I listened. I suggested she give it time. You are newlyweds. You both are older and set in your ways. It will be an adjustment. I tried to provide comfort, but I felt awful for her. As time went on, things would go up and down. After my niece was born, they moved back to Louisiana to live near family. Married life seemed to be better for her at times and having a daughter kept her busy. Throughout the years and with all of the counseling, things were not better in her marriage or much different than they were in the beginning. It broke my heart to see my sister hurting. She would say, "I want us to break the generational curse of divorce." She carried this pressure on her shoulders. She did everything she could to save that marriage, but was holding on because she did not want to be divorced. She honestly felt like because our grandparents and parents were divorced, if she got a divorce, a curse would continue. Meanwhile, her daughter was seeing their marriage. Would she think that is what marriage should be like? Would she want the opposite based on her negative connections? Was she even recognizing it as a negative connection since she was only nine years old? Or would she accept the same because that is all she knew?

Tricia divorced a little over a year ago. I'm not writing to give advice on divorce and whether or not your divorce or any other divorce is justified. I do, however, believe that Tricia wanted opposite of what my parents had and was willing to do anything and everything to stay married and not get divorced. She had a negative connection to my parent's divorce and because of that she did not want her child to go through the same experience.

Let's move on to Scott. He had a girlfriend for six months. As the relationship progressed and time passed he was getting scared. He broke up with her. Our phone rang at 2:00 a.m. It was my brother wanting to talk to my husband, Jim. He was very upset. They talked for a while. Scott was fearful of getting married. Scott was fearful of having children. He told Jim that he didn't want to turn out like our dad. He didn't want to get married or have children because he didn't want to hurt anyone. All of his life he had been told, "You look just like your daddy. You are just like him too." I do not believe family and friends knew how this impacted Scott emotionally. I didn't. He internalized his feelings, all the while believing he would become who my dad was back then. Dad played all of the sports when he was growing up. Scott played them too. They looked alike. They both had a temper at times. You get the idea. He thought if everyone is saying he was just like him, then he must be, and with all vices included. Scott asked Jim how he got through his own parent's divorce. Jim said, "I am my own man. I am who I want to be. You are your own man. You need to choose who you want to be." Jim also told Scott that he was basing his fear on our dad and his experiences, and reminded Scott that Pop has been a wonderful example of how a husband and dad should be. Jim asked him, "Do you love her?" Scott said, "Yes." They got back together and eventually were married.

In this situation, Scott initially had a negative connection to an experience, and wanted nothing to do with it. Fear of becoming what he knew paralyzed him. Paralyzed him so much so that he focused on the negative experiences with our dad and what he didn't have with him versus the positive experiences with Pop.

Earlier, I said that parents make choices each and every day. Every person, regardless of their role, makes choices each and every day. I am a daughter, mother, wife, granddaughter, friend, sibling, co-worker, cousin, volunteer, etc. I strive to be my best, and, in turn, I hope it makes a difference in my children and the people around me. I am this way because I choose to be this way. I want others to have positive connections in our experiences shared. What they do with those experiences is up to them. I hope to be known for what I represent versus what I do not represent. Would you rather hear your child say, "I want to be just like you when I grow up" or "I do not want to be anything like you when I grow up"?

It is very emotional to think of the impact we have on our children. You can choose to have a positive impact on your children's lives daily.

Open MIC Session

Adam is not married and none of his siblings are married. They are all still young and haven't shared what their expectations will be yet of their future spouses. After seeing his mom go through this, he will not cheat. His dad cheating and withdrawing have been his negative connections to his experiences thus far.

Barbara has been married for over twenty-two years and counting. Her brother has been married several years as well.

Carrie has been married for over twenty-four years. She and her husband had incredibly similar childhoods. They decided before they got married that they would never put their children through what they went through. He was the first person she dated. When they would have an argument or disagreement, she would think he was going to bail on the relationship. It took time for her to be confident and believe he loved her unconditionally. She finally realized that not all men leave and not all marriages are fleeting.

Chapter 19

NEVER GIVE UP OR QUIT!

"There is no failure except in no longer trying."
- Elbert Hubbard

I remember Mom telling me that if I started something, whether it was a softball season or a band year, I had to finish it. I was not allowed to commit to a team or group and then quit. She explained to me the importance of seeing it through until the end. When I was a pitcher in softball I witnessed something traumatic. We were playing another team and one of our girls hit the ball and hot-lined the pitcher right in the face. She fell to the ground on the pitcher's mound and was hurt badly. She was crying and her parents came out to meet the coach to take her off the field.

My fear got the best of me. I was scared to death to go out the next inning and pitch. My legs were shaking and I was not pitching many strikes. The umpire called "Ball" several times and the girls walked to first base. My coach came to talk to me on the pitcher's mound and asked me if I was okay and what was going on. I told him I was scared now. He took me out of the game, thank goodness, and I sat on the bench for the first time all season.

Later that night, at home, I told my parents that I did not want to play anymore. They couldn't believe it. We talked and I explained that seeing the other player get hot-lined was scary. How could I continue to pitch after seeing that injury? What if that happens to me? They told me that I could not quit the team. The team and coach were depending on me this season. After I finish the season, and before the next season began, I could decide if I wanted to play softball again. "Is this fair?" I thought. "Do my parents even care if I get hurt? Why would they continue to make me play and be on the team?"

I told myself that I could go to practices, not do well, and then the coach wouldn't play me in the games. Well, that did not work for me. My coach lined us all up and one by one whether we were a pitcher or not, we had to get on the pitcher's mound and field the softballs hit by our teammates. He explained that he knew it was scary for each one of us to see the other player get hurt and this would help us understand that out of hundreds of hits, getting hot-lined is rare.

It was my turn. Oh happy day. Not! I get on the pitcher's mound and no one other than the best and hardest hitter on our team gets up to the plate. Really? This is who I have to pitch to? I was trembling and a nervous wreck. I hesitantly pitched the ball and it was not in the strike zone. I pitch again, she hits the ball, and as it is coming right to me I bend over and put my glove in from of my face. The ball goes off to the side. How embarrassing! I went on and pitched more to her and eventually realized I would be okay. If this was our biggest and hardest hitter, one of the best in the league—an All-star player, I could do it. I made it through several hits and didn't get hot-lined. Coaches are good and typically know what they are doing. He needed me to see for myself that there was nothing to fear. I would not even have had that chance if my parents did not force me to keep my commitment and stay on the team. Quitting was not an option in my family. Giving up was not an option in my family.

Much like this example with my softball team, quitting parenting is not an option. Giving up as a parent is not an option. Your team is your family. You must see it through the season, and the season is a lifetime. Children will still be your children no matter what their age is. And you will still be their parent no matter how old you are.

TIP: Keep your commitment as a parent, and do not give up!

It is ironic to me that I tell my children a lot of the same things my parents told me. They were valuable lessons then and still are today. Time and time again we have to remind our children that if they start something they must finish it. When they were younger they wanted to try so many different sports and activities. Eventually, we figured that they would find one they liked and stick to it longer than one season and they both did. Until that time came it was a hoot!

Our youngest son was extremely interested in playing soccer; he was only six years old at the time. This was his first "real commitment" with a sport. The kids out there looked so cute. They would all run in a group back and forth on the soccer field at practice. Their cheeks were red and hair was a sweaty hot mess. They learned some techniques, but really how much can a six year old learn? They are like sponges I know, but their attention span is not like ours. It was funny. He would come home worn out from practice in the evenings. His first game day arrived! The entire family comes out with their chairs, bottled waters, umbrellas, and cameras. We had a late morning game. In South Louisiana, it gets extremely hot and the humidity is at least 90%. The umbrellas were not used to protect us from the rain, but from the sun. My freckles were connecting as each minute ticked away.

The little soccer players ran back and forth. Similar to practices, they would run in groups. They were talking, laughing, and sometimes would just stop and stand in the field until they felt like running again or until the coach would yell and wake them up from daydreaming.

He makes it through the game. Everyone is cheering for these six-year-olds, and we make a tunnel with our arms reached over for them to run through. He goes to the tent to pick up his sports drink and snack. You know nowadays there is always a snack sign-up sheet! He runs over and we all get our hugs and congratulate him on his first game. We say our good-byes to family and we head home. One our way home, I asked him to tell me his favorite part of the game. He said, "The snacks!" He continued, "It is too hot! I am done with this soccer!

It is too much work!" Needless to say at six years old, he had a life lesson on keeping his commitments, not giving up, and that quitting was not an option, which was much like the discussion my parents had with me.

At the age of forty-four years old, I still have to remind myself that I must keep my commitments and quitting is not an option. It helped me as a child, as an adult, as a parent, as a worker, in my faith, and in my relationships.

I grew up as a worker bee. We were taught to work hard. I started babysitting at twelve years old and did that for years. In my senior year of high school, at the age of sixteen, I was in the Cooperative Education Program. I attended my high school classes until 11:30 a.m. and then worked at an insurance agency from 12:00 p.m. until 5:30 p.m. Monday – Friday. The program taught me business etiquette, typing, interview skills, communication skills, and many other important skills. Our supervisors would report to our teacher on how we were doing in the workplace and she would go over our evaluations with us individually. I did great and soon after starting the job I took on more responsibilities. The agent then asked me to work full-time during the summer, so I did. She knew I would be leaving in July to go to college, so she called an insurance agent in the college town and told him he needed to hire me. I worked there too once I went to college. I graduated in eight semesters and found a job right away. I worked for twenty years and advanced in my career with each position. I worked for a non-profit organization, publicly traded corporations, and privately held companies. Thirteen of which were for the same company. I loved it. I was loyal. My work ethic was exceptional. I always met or exceeded expectations. We were acquired by another company. I made it through the first round of lay-offs. Six months later, the Chief Executive Officer was laid off, along with all of his leadership team members, which included me. I was the only one they asked to stay another two weeks. Of course I said, "Yes." I prepared a transition plan that was several full pages. I worked my fingers to the bone to do as much as I could before I left.

I took time off at the holidays and end of the year and started a new job with similar duties. After six months, my supervisor tells me that the owner may lay off people from each department. He wanted to give me professional courtesy so I could start looking for another job. He wrote a recommendation, just like my last supervisor had, and I found another job in my career field.

After seven months of working there I was laid off. My supervisor felt badly, but it was out of her control. The company was not doing well financially and more lay-offs were forthcoming. I just had my six month performance evaluation and was doing great. I also received an annual salary increase the month prior to the lay-off. I was back on the market. If any of you have ever changed jobs, you know how much of an adjustment it is each time.

After working twenty years and never being laid off, I had now been laid off three times in one and half years. What do you think I did? Do you think I gave up? Do you believe I quit looking for a job? I kept searching for a job. I will not lie and say it was not difficult. I was on and off the market now three times, at no fault of my own, yet I was beating myself up thinking if there was anything I could have done differently. I am one of the best employees a company can have on staff. Why was this happening to me AGAIN? What was God trying to teach me by these experiences? Was I being tested? With everything going on in my life professionally and personally, I prayed to God one day and said, "Okay. I get it. I've learned so many things. I'm ready to be done with my storm."

I had to update all of my accounts used for job searching: LinkedIn, Indeed, ZipRecruiter, Experteer, etc. When I updated my LinkedIn account I felt embarrassed and like a job hopper. I continued to search, but what got me through it is believing that everything happens for a reason and submersing myself in watching an old television show, Murder She Wrote, starring Angela Lansbury. Go ahead and pause for your laughter! I know it is corny, but I love that television show. What I love most about the character, Jessica Fletcher, is not just her cool accent, but her tenacity. She never gives up! If something didn't sit right with her about a murder, she kept searching for clues and kept trying her best until she figured it out. For the first two months, I would wake up in the morning, drink my coffee, watch the show, and then look on all of the job search engines.

There are so many blessings I have identified from reflection during this time off, and many lessons learned. More than you have time for, as so much has transpired over the last several months. I will leave the details for my next book. God has His own timing and reasons for this time off in between jobs. One of which was to write this book. I am starting a new job soon and will be a worker bee again. I am excited. I am energized. I am refreshed to begin something new and challenging.

Just as we tell our children not to give up or quit, I am telling you not to give up or quit. No matter how high you think this mountain is it is not high enough for you to quit. There are no mountains too high to climb for yourself and your children.

According to the Guinness World Records' website, Mt. Everest located in Nepal is the highest mountain in the world with its peak being 29,028 feet 9 inches, which is the highest point and has the highest altitude in the world. Can you imagine climbing that mountain? I think about how exhausting that must be, much less how dangerous it seems. I am certain I would be out of breath, having muscle cramps in my fingers, arms and legs, back pain, cracked lips, and feel like my feet were going to fall off. What makes it worth climbing Mt. Everest? What makes it worth climbing your mountain right now? What is your reward? Who comes running to you when the theme song from Rocky, the 1976 movie, is played?

The relationships with your children are your reward. Your reward is knowing you never stopped trying to be there for them and you most certainly did not quit. Your reward is feeling at peace with your decisions and confident you did your best for yourself and your children. You will not receive a big, shiny, gold star for your accomplishments and being a parent. You will receive a special place in your children's hearts and a relationship that will outlast time. Isn't that worth your struggles? Isn't that worth your climb?

Chapter 20

WHERE ARE WE NOW?

"So now faith, hope, and love abide, these three; but the greatest of these is love."-1 Corinthians 13:13 (ESV)

Love is powerful. Love is the light. Love conquers all. Love is the answer.

My relationships with my parents are wonderful. I have all of them in my life, each in a unique and special role. I love them very much and am honored to be their daughter.

Mom and Pop recently celebrated their thirtieth wedding anniversary. I see them often, as they only live one mile away. I am still amazed by Mom frequently. She continues to be a constant reminder of the mom I hope I am to my boys. Pop... He is a man who changed my life. He is a true example of how a father should be. He filled a void in my heart and life that I will never be able to repay him for through words or deeds. I am still in awe of him, and I should be. He chose to say yes to us children when he had an opportunity not to. He was selfless then and is selfless now. For that and much more, I am forever grateful.

Dad and Veda celebrated their twenty-eighth wedding anniversary this year. They live about ten minutes from me. They are retired, but continue to be very involved in their church and have started a ministry (www.immanuelhealsministry.com). Veda continues to amaze me on how graceful she is. As for Dad, he is spiritual, funny, loud, and a hoot to be around. He still loves to preach! Dad and I have a special bond now that I appreciate and treasure. I love them both, and I know they love me and my family.

All of my parents are able to be around each other and attend family parties and events. My boys are able to have their grandparents together with no issues or concerns at their programs and functions. We all love each other. At birthday dinners and other special events, I find myself looking around at all of them and living in that moment. My heart is full. I could not imagine my life any other way. I am grateful. I am humbled. I am blessed.

All of my parents are living examples of how marriage should be. Seeing them happy, laughing, loving, and living brings me joy! I see positive traits in both relationships that continue to encourage me in my own marriage.

Jim and I have been married for over twenty years. Our marriage is healthy and growing stronger each day as we go through raising teenage boys and travel through this journey we call life. We are far from perfect, but are perfect for each other. When I reach a point where I think I could not love him any more than I do in that moment, I realize I love him even more. I wrote him a love poem and presented it to him at our wedding rehearsal dinner on August 27, 1999. It hangs in our home so beautifully, and is a constant reminder of my love for him and the commitment we made so many years ago. The commitment of our marriage will always be a priority. It is written in calligraphy and is matted and framed. I still get chill bumps and am moved when I read it because our love is even deeper than it was in the beginning.

I would like to share it with you now:

PLEASE DON'T DIVORCE ME

There are so many feelings I would like to share,

but below are a few that will show you how much I care.

You are the sunshine in all of my days,

and you make me glow in a very special way.

The way you talk to me makes me want to melt.

and your touch is always as soft as felt.

Your laughter is frequent, and that's what I need.

You see, laughter is contagious and spreads like a weed.

When you hold me I feel safe and secure,

and your words are always sweet and pure.

Like a flower, our relationship will continue to blossom,

and with you in my life it couldn't be more awesome.

VICKIE HALL

*I especially love your big
brown eyes,*

*because when I look into them
I feel as high as the sky.*

*I love you with all of my heart
and soul.*

*My love for you burns like the
fire on coal.*

*I look forward to spending the
rest of my life with you.*

*We will make many memories,
and grow old together too.*

*I thank God every day for
blessing me with you,*

*what more can I ask for than
my dream come true.*

You are the love of my life,

*and in just one more day I will
be your wife.*

With all my love,

Vickie

My sister, Tricia, is doing fine. She is happier and continues to work through things after her recent divorce. She and her ex-husband share custody (50/50) of my niece and strive to continue to make her the focus as they move forward. She has maintained relationships with his side of the family and wants nothing more than for them to be a part of her life. She seems to be passed the worry of the "generational curse" pressure she put on herself for all of these years.

My brother, Scott, is also doing well. He and his wife celebrated their sixteenth wedding anniversary this year. They have two daughters. When I look at my baby brother, I am so happy and proud that he became his own man. He decided who he wanted to be as a husband and as a father and strives to do his best. He would not be happy if he expected anything less of himself.

Open MIC Session

Adam has a great relationship with his mom. His family is really close and tell each other everything. With his dad he still feels hurt, aggravated, and stressed. He continues to question his dad's love for him. He doesn't know if their relationship will ever be fixed.

> **Advice for parents: Give your children compliments when they accomplish things and be there when they are down. They need you!**

Barbara doesn't have anything else to share, as it's too painful. Her overall relationship with her parents consists of no relationship with her father, and she is the caregiver of her mom.

Carrie's relationship with her parents is good, sometimes even great. She and her father have gotten really close in the latter years, and it's a relationship she always longed to have with him. She feels like the "third time is a charm" for her parents and does not believe there will be a fourth marriage. Everyone gets along nicely and it is drama free!

Chapter 21

CONCLUSION

"A new door cannot be opened until you have the courage to close the one behind you." - www.dailyinspirationalquotes.com

I did not have horrific stories to share, because there weren't any. My parents fell in love, got married, had children, and remained married for fifteen years. They divorced. My relationship with my dad became distant over a short time in my mind. He wasn't attentive and involved. We grew apart. My mom married Pop, and I felt like I had a family again. My dad married Veda and they were a happy couple. I saw my dad and Veda for birthdays and holidays. Later in life, when I was an adult, and my son was 4 years old, I started to become closer to my dad. We have a special bond again and for that I am grateful.

The church I said I would never step foot in again…Well, my family started going there. We continued to attend church there until about one and half years after my dad retired as a Pastor. God brought me full circle didn't he? I smile when I think of it all.

The divorce was not easy. No one's divorce is easy. I cried rivers (not just one river) of tears and fought with my emotions daily; but as time passed, hearts healed and relationships were restored. I realized as I grew older, that all of my parents did the best they could at the time and with the knowledge at hand. Most of all, they did love me. No one is perfect, and the flaws we witness in our parents are in us too. I love my life and appreciate how and when everything happened. I have many happy memories and continue to make them daily. If anything had changed, I wouldn't be who I am today, nor would I have the special people now in my life from my "bonus" families. I am overwhelmed with all of the blessings, love, and grace that have been bestowed on our family. #blessedbeyondmeasure

My sister described it best in a paper she wrote in high school. The topic had to be about something she thought was bad, but turned out to be good. She used the analogy of our family tree being struck by lighting and dying, but as time went on and our parents re-married, we were able to add even more branches to our family tree. It wasn't dying. It was making room for growth.

It is possible to have a happily ever after ending for you and your family. Write your own story and choose your own ending. You have control over this divorce and how it impacts you and your children. Look forward and not behind you.

In this guide you have read my personal story, along with three other children's stories. I also included some of the feelings of my sister and brother to illustrate the different perceptions of children based on age and knowledge. You have also been provided tips to help you remember, in a nutshell, suggestions of what to do or how to respond during each phase identified in the chapters:

TIP #1: Parents are our first true loves, so do not tell your children, "We fell out of love." or "We do not love each other anymore." Children cannot process these words or change of emotion. To them, this just happened overnight, regardless of whether or not you have been having issues for a while. Children will start to question, "Can they fall out of love with me too?" This creates a nervous feeling and more anxiety of what is to come in the future with their parent/child relationship.

TIP #2: Seek counseling for your children. Find a counselor that you are comfortable with, whether it is a local practice, at church, or elsewhere. Do not allow your children to make this decision, as they do not know what is best for them. Children should not dictate adult decisions.

TIP #3: Seek counseling for yourself and remember, your children are not your counselors.

TIP #4: Do not speak negatively about the other parent. If you do not have anything positive or supportive to say, then keep quiet.

TIP #5: Be mindful of how you approach your children

with of any new habits and/or ways of living. Think about how you are going to incorporate those changes when you are with your children.

TIP #6: Keep in contact with the in-laws (aunts, uncles, cousins, grandparents). Schedule times for you to bring the kids to visit their family members, even if it's on "your days."

TIP #7: Make it a priority to attend your children's events and functions. If you are physically able to go and can take off of work, then go!

TIP #8: Stay connected with your children. Call them as often as possible, even if it's just to say, "Hi, I love you! How was your day? Good night and sweet dreams!"

TIP #9: Take time to integrate your children with your future spouse and their families. This should not be rushed. It shows the children how important being a family is, and that everyone knows each other and feels comfortable and accepted.

TIP #10: Strive to discuss plans privately, at least in the beginning, for cohesion. Try to avoid saying, "Yours, Mine, and Ours". Children could interpret such as some are more important than others based on who they biologically belong to.

TIP #11: Work with your children to understand forgiveness and what it means for them. There is not a timeframe on when forgiveness comes for the ones who have hurt you or you have hurt. I encourage you to aim for sooner rather than later.

TIP #12: Do not allow statistics to bring you down. Use them to fuel the love for yourself and children, as well as motivation to ensure your family does not become a negative statistic.

TIP #13: Choose happiness and love.

TIP #14: Do not allow this divorce to affect you in a way that risks your child's innocence of who you are and what you would do for them.

TIP #15: You cannot force your children to communicate with you. You can, however, constantly reinforce to them that they can tell you anything (along with any parameters you feel necessary) and ensure they feel safe to do so.

TIP #16: Child support does not need to be discussed with your children. It is a legal obligation and an adult topic of discussion.

TIP #17: Communicate with the other parent on what the response should be, just as you did when you were married, especially on big purchases. Ensure alignment on what you both feel the children should have or shouldn't have.

TIP #18: Do your best to confirm your children understand your words and actions. For example, you could ask, "Did you understand what I meant when I said XYZ? It seems as though you are upset. Let's talk more about it." Or "Do you understand why I couldn't be there or XYZ?"

TIP #19: Make a daily choice to be your best in all that you do! Focus on the positive in all things.

TIP #20: Keep your commitment as a parent, and do not give up!

As we went through each chapter, I am sure you noticed that several of the topics interweaved some way or another. For example, the better the communication is between you and your children, there may be an increase in the probability that their perception is more aligned to what you intended them to receive from your words or actions. Sufficient counseling for all involved could lead to forgiveness sooner rather than later. Showing up for your children and staying connected between visits could result in a better relationship. Love and happiness will shine brighter than negativity and a bad attitude. Each TIP provided has brought you closer to connecting all of the dots as you move forward. If you take away and implement one positive tip it will be better for you and your children's relationships.

You have a great starting point to make this a better divorce. When I hear people say, "There's another divorce… another broken home," I cringe. The marital relationship is over with your spouse, but your home is not broken, and you still need to have a relationship with your spouse for parenting purposes. Continue to keep your family (you and your children) fixed and together to ensure they do not become emotionally broken. A home is where you are and the memories you share with your children are made. Please do not become a victim because of this divorce, instead create your own victory. Like I said earlier, it is not always pretty, but it doesn't have to be ugly either. Give your children what they need. Give them you, your love, and your support. Give them your best!

You've got this! Divorce does not have to be a crutch for you and your children. It doesn't have to ruin your lives either. Do not allow this divorce to define you and your children. Make it better for them. Make it right for them. Make it the best situation possible considering the circumstances. Do whatever you can so your children know they are loved, supported, and protected. Your actions will dictate how your relationship with your children will be going forward. Make it positive ones!

Again, you are your children's first true loves. You are the best examples they have on how they will expect to be treated in the future in any relationship. I did not write this book to tell you how to parent your children. There is no book that will tell you everything you need to know on that subject. No parent is perfect and we all make mistakes. My hope is that you take away tips that will help you in making decisions regarding your children and possibly understand how they are processing their emotions as they go through the divorce. Their understanding and perceptions are completely different than yours. Recognize it, address it, and move forward in your journey. Many parents have paved the way before you, and I believe we all learn by sharing our stories. As Maya Angelou so eloquently said, "Do the best you can until you know better. Then when you know better, do better."

I know, without a doubt, divorce can be better for everyone involved, especially the children. Make yours better starting today!

A NOTE FROM THE AUTHOR

I wrote this book as a passion project to advocate for all children and families. Once I became older, I realized there is a huge gap between what parents say and do versus how a child perceives those words and actions, especially during a divorce and the aftermath. Situations come up that are unlike a family with parents who are not divorced. It led me to share my story based on my experiences and feelings as a child having divorced parents. I was angry, confused, devastated, embarrassed, hurt, and on an emotional roller coaster for a long time. I couldn't understand why my life changed and why my relationships changed. My first two true loves broke my heart into many pieces, and I didn't think my heart would ever be put back together.

The reason I shared about the divorce specifically is because that is what I went through with my family. I am able to identify and share

NOTE FROM AUTHOR

how I felt and my perceptions as a child to illustrate examples of just how different a child and parent think when those sticky situations come up. The family has to learn an entirely different routine and way of life. I have also been able to recognize as an adult that it was never my parents' intentions to hurt me in any way. When I became a parent myself, it bumped the level of emotion and understanding to a whole new level. Part of me could not imagine ever saying "those words" or not being there for my children. The other part of me had to take a step back and truly recognize that parents are doing the best they can with what they know how to do in that moment and based on their well-being. I wanted to cut parents some slack, because I was a parent; I was imperfect; I was doing my best. And what if it wasn't enough for my family? What did that say about me? But, wait a minute and pause at that statement. It stopped me in my tracks. I didn't recognize this until I was an adult, over the age of 30, and a parent myself after hearts were healed.

The point being is that a child does not comprehend words and interpret actions or inactions the way an adult processes them. A child does not have adult reasoning and understanding. Recognizing this will help you and your family, and that is what my hope is! That is the purpose of this book. None of this is the child's responsibility. Children learn the "who, what, when and how" from the parents.

NOTE FROM AUTHOR

My heart was put back together many years ago. Relationships were restored and our family dynamic has been changed forever.

Learn from the families that have paved the way for you, divorced parents or not! Learn from my family, as we all learn from each other's life experiences. Children are just that, children. Be there. Love them. Protect them. Support them. Leave no room for doubt. They need you in their lives, and they need to be a priority. Family is a priority.

Please don't divorce your children.

Much Love,
Vickie

ACKNOWLEDGEMENTS

First and foremost, I would like to thank God for the strength and courage to write this book, and discernment as I recalled memories and experiences from my childhood through today.

I would like to thank all of my parents for their love and support throughout my life and my children's lives. We have a special family, and I am grateful for where we are today in our relationships.

Thank you to my husband, Jim, and my sons, Brandon and Nathan. You inspire me every day to be a better Christian, woman, wife, and mother. I love you and appreciate your patience and support as I wrote this book. Your encouragement has been amazing!

A huge thank you goes out to my book club ladies who encouraged me throughout this process and helped me believe I could do it! It was our first book eight months ago that asked, "If there was

ACKNOWLEDGEMENTS

anything you could do and not fail what would it be?" And here I am, ladies! I have succeeded just by writing it and followed my heart. #girlcode

Shout out to the three children who shared their stories with me for the "Open MIC Sessions" and my sister, Tricia, and brother, Scott, for allowing me to share their feelings and experiences. Parents will not only hear my story, but they will also hear part of yours too. I am extremely grateful for your contributions.

I would like to thank Michelle Jester for her amazing guidance during this project. We connected from the first day we met. She is not only a gifted author and consultant, she is a compassionate woman who provides support and love to everyone around her. MJ, you have my sincerest appreciation and gratitude for all you have done with helping me share my story.

Readers, thank you for taking the time to read my book. I hope it touches your life in a positive way and helps you during this difficult time. Feel free to email me directly with your feedback at authorvickiehall@gmail.com.

ABOUT THE AUTHOR

Vickie grew up in a small town in Louisiana. She graduated with a degree in Business Administration and played in the college marching and symphony bands to foster her love for music since fifth grade. Vickie has been married for over twenty years to the love of her life and best friend. She and her husband have two sons. They have shared in the joys and tears of raising boys and refer to themselves as the "A-Team". One is going to college in the fall and "half" of the empty nest will begin! Her youngest son is in high school.

By day, Vickie has enjoyed a 24-year career in

ABOUT THE AUTHOR

contracts management and operations and by night has written many poems and cards and scrapbooks to capture fun memories. She loves spending time with family and friends!

She is known for and recognized by many traits, but freckles, red hair, loud sneezes, compassion, love and laughter tops the list. She is also the Co-founder and President of Krewe de Halcyon, a social organization dedicated to positively impacting the community and embracing the Louisiana tradition of Mardi Gras (one of her favorite holidays!)

Also from Rope Swing Publishing

Inside her father's old weathered barn, Eve and her siblings find an old tarnished tool box that sits waiting for them as their father languishes in the hospital. To most, the items in the box would be considered insignificant junk, but to Eve they held priceless insight into not only the man her father was, but also the woman she was about to become.

From a very delicate relationship with her mom as a teenager, to being forced to live with her father in a town she never felt at home in, Eve learned to grow and live. When adversity hits through both tragedy and disappointment Eve soon finds the strength to push to survive.

With the help of the items in the toolbox, Eve is beset with uncovering the treasures it holds…ones that propel her on a journey of self-discovery and revelations.

A mysterious letter arrives from America to the village of Highland Way, where Annie, the oldest daughter in the Ewing Family was left to care for her mother and younger sister after her father left to find work in Dublin. Soon, Annie, Lily, and Katy find themselves on a harrowing journey.

The handwritten note not only will expose deep secrets, it will also challenge the strength and fortitude of the Ewing women, leading each member into their own soul searching voyage.

Follow this extraordinary passage that begins in Ireland and leads each woman to uncover their own courage and truths in this new world.

Olivia Brooks has been able to keep her life in Sugar Mill, Louisiana held perfectly together, far away from the small town where she grew up. Even though her past still haunts her, she has found a perfect process of surviving, until a string of events brings Luke Plaisance to Sugar Mill and turns her organized life upside down.

While Olivia fights to hold on to the life she's created, unraveling it may be exactly what it takes for her to truly survive. She must accept her past in order to live, or let it threaten the only future she's ever wanted. Because some secrets can't stay buried… and shouldn't.

An inspiring and heartbreaking tale of abandonment, survival, and purpose. A harrowing journey of self-discovery and perseverance.

NOTES

NOTES

www.ingramcontent.com/pod-product-compliance
Lightning Source LLC
LaVergne TN
LVHW041541070426
835507LV00011B/867